BEST-LOVED
Prayers
&
Blessings

Publications International, Ltd.

Louis Weber, CEO
Publications International, Ltd.
8140 Lehigh Avenue
Morton Grove, Illinois 60053

ISBN: 978-1-68022-322-4

Manufactured in China.

8 7 6 5 4 3 2 1

Table of Contents

Psalm 145:18 says, "The Lord is nigh unto all them that call upon him, to all that call upon him in truth." What a beautiful promise that is. It reminds us that we are called to a closer relationship with God through prayer and assures us that God is always listening.

Prayer can take many forms—from casual, spontaneous prayer to the singing of well-loved hymns to quiet reflection. We know that if we are sincere, all of these forms are pleasing to God. In *Best-Loved Prayers and Blessings*, we've gathered an assortment of traditional, well-loved prayers, blessings, hymns, Bible verses, psalms, poems, and reflections. When you're looking for words, just navigate to the relevant chapter and flip through until the right words catch your eye. In the first two chapters, "Prayers and Blessings for Daily Life" and "Prayers and Blessings for Special Occasions," you'll find blessings that you can use for your family and friends on many different occasions. Calling on God to bless someone is a powerful gift to give your children, spouse, or friends. Later chapters explore different themes, from praise and thanksgiving to repentance and forgiveness to prayer itself.

And when you've looking for words, never forget that sometimes the simplest words are best. If you are short on time or words, you can always echo these short proclamations of belief and trust from the Bible:

• The words of Peter: "Thou art the Christ, the Son of the living God." (Matthew 16:16)

• The words of a father asking Jesus to help his son: "Lord, I believe; help thou mine unbelief." (Mark 9:24)

• The words of the blind man: "Jesus, thou son of David, have mercy on me." (Luke 18:38)

• The words of Thomas: "My Lord and my God." (John 20:28)

Before Prayer

I weave a silence on my lips,
I weave a silence into my mind,
I weave a silence within my heart.
I close my ears to distractions,
I close my eyes to attentions,
I close my heart to temptations.
Calm me, O Lord, as you stilled the storm,
Still me, O Lord, keep me from harm.
Let all the tumult within me cease,
Enfold me, Lord, in your peace.

—**Celtic Traditional**

Prayers and Blessings for Daily Life

W̶e are God's children, called to communion with him. Daily prayer helps us draw close to God. In this section you'll find prayers that are perfect for morning, evening, and throughout the day, as well as prayers and Bible verses that you can use to bless family and friends at any time.

Morning Prayers

G ive ear to my words, O Lord,
consider my meditation.
Hearken unto the voice of my cry, my King,
and my God: for unto thee will I pray.
My voice shalt thou hear in the morning,
O Lord; in the morning will I direct my prayer
unto thee, and will look up.

—Psalm 5:1–3

New Every Morning

New every morning is the love
Our wakening and uprising prove;
Through sleep and darkness safely brought,
Restored to life and power and thought.

New mercies, each returning day,
Hover around us while we pray;
New perils past, new sins forgiven,
New thoughts of God, new hopes of heaven.

Prepare, O Lord, in your dear love,
for perfect life with you above;
and help us, this and every day,
to live more nearly as we pray.

—John Keble

A Child's Prayer for Morning

Now, before I run to play,
Let me not forget to pray
To God who kept me through the night
And waked me with the morning light.
Help me, Lord, to love thee more
Than I ever loved before,
In my work and in my play
Be thou with me through the day.
Amen.

—Author Unknown

Evening Prayers

Into thy hands, O Father and Lord, we commend this night, ourselves, our families and friends, all those we love and those who love us, all folk rightly believing, and all who need thy pity and protection: light us with thy holy grace, and suffer us never to be separated from thee, O Lord in Trinity, God everlasting.

—St. Edmund Rich, Archbishop of Canterbury

O Lord God, who has given us the night for rest, I pray that in my sleep my soul may remain awake to you, steadfastly adhering to your love. As I lay aside my cares to relax and relieve my mind, may I not forget your infinite and

unresting care for me. And in this way, let my conscience be at peace, so that when I rise tomorrow, I am refreshed in body, mind and soul.

—John Calvin

Watch, dear Lord, with those who wake,
or watch, or weep tonight, and give your
angels charge over those who sleep.
Tend your sick ones, O Lord Christ,
Rest your weary ones.
Bless your dying ones.
Soothe your suffering ones.
Pity your afflicted ones.
Shield your joyous ones.
And all for your love's sake.
Amen.

—St. Augustine

Children's Bedtime Prayer

Now I lay me down to sleep,
I pray the Lord my soul to keep:
May God guard me through the night
And wake me with the morning light.
Amen.

—Traditional

Lighten our darkness, Lord, we pray; and in your mercy defend us from all perils and dangers of this night; for the love of your only Son, our Savior Jesus Christ. Amen.

—Gelasian Sacramentary

May you have warm words on a cold evening,
a full moon on a dark night,
and a smooth road all the way to your door.

—Irish Traditional

Prayers for the Day

Father, We Thank Thee

F ather, we thank thee for the night,
  And for the pleasant morning light;
   For rest and food and loving care,
And all that makes the day so fair.

Help us to do the things we should,
To be to others kind and good;
In all we do, in work or play,
To grow more loving every day.

—Rebecca Weston

Night and day may we give you praise and thanks, because you have shown us that all things belong to you, and all blessings are gifts from you.

—Clement of Alexandria

Keep me at evening,
Keep me at morning,
Keep me at noon.
I am tired,
astray and stumbling,
shield me from sin.

—Celtic Traditional

O may thy spirit guide my feet
In ways of righteousness;
Make every path of duty straight,
And plain before my face.
Amen.

—**Joachim Neander**

B less to me, O God, the earth beneath my feet,
Bless to me, O God, the path whereon I go,
Bless to me, O God, the people whom I meet,
Today, tonight and tomorrow.

—**Celtic Traditional**

O most merciful Redeemer, friend, and brother;
may we know Thee more clearly,
love Thee more dearly,
and follow Thee more nearly,
day by day.

—Richard of Chichester

May the good saints protect you
And bless you today,
And may trouble ignore you
Each step of the way.

—Irish Traditional

Lord, may I be wakeful at sunrise to begin a new day for you, cheerful at sunset for having done my work for you; thankful at moonrise and under starshine for the beauty of the universe. And may I add what little may be in me to your great world.

—The Abbot of Greve

St. Patrick's Breastplate

I bind unto myself today
the strong name of the Trinity
by invocation of the same,
the Three in One
and One in Three.

I bind this day
to me forever,
by power of faith,
Christ's
incarnation,
his baptism in
the Jordan river,
his death on cross
for my salvation,
his bursting from
the spiced tomb,
his riding up the
heavenly way,
his coming at the day of doom,
I bind unto myself today.

I bind unto myself today
the virtues of the starlit heaven,
the glorious sun's life-giving ray,

the whiteness of the moon at even,
the flashing of the lightning free,
the whirling wind's tempestuous shocks,
the stable earth, the deep salt sea
around the old eternal rocks.

I bind unto myself today
the power of God to hold and lead,
God's eye to watch, God's might to stay,
God's ear to hearken to my need,
the wisdom of my God to teach,
God's hand to guide, God's shield to ward,
the word of God to give me speech,
God's heavenly host to be my guard.

Christ be with me, Christ within me,
Christ behind me, Christ before me,
Christ beside me, Christ to win me,
Christ to comfort and restore me.

Christ beneath me, Christ above me,
Christ in quiet, Christ in danger,
Christ in hearts of all that love me,
Christ in mouth of friend and stranger.

I bind unto myself the name,
the strong name of the Trinity
by invocation of the same,
the Three in One and One in Three,
of whom all nature has creation,
eternal Father, Spirit, Word.
Praise to the Lord of my salvation;
salvation is of Christ the Lord!

—Attributed to St. Patrick,
trans. Cecil Francis Alexander

Blessings for Meals

B less us, oh Lord,
and these thy gifts
which we are about to receive
from thy bounty,
through Christ, our Lord.
Amen.

—Traditional

We Give Our Thanks

F or food that stays our hunger,
For rest that brings us ease,
For homes where memories linger,
We give our thanks for these.

—Traditional

General Blessings

May the blessing of light be on you, light without and light within. May the blessed sunshine shine on you and warm your heart till it glows like a great peat fire, so that the stranger may come and warm himself at it, and also a friend.

—**Traditional Irish**

May the babe of Bethlehem be yours to tend;
May the Boy of Nazareth be yours for friend;
May the Man of Galilee his healing send;
May the Christ of Calvary his courage lend;
May the Risen Lord his presence send;
And his holy angels defend you to the end.

—"Pilgrim's Prayer,"
found in Oberammergau, Germany

May the fire of this log
warm the cold;
may the hungry be fed;
may the weary find rest,
and may all enjoy Heaven's peace.

—Traditional

May there always be work for your hands to do.
May your purse always hold a coin or two.
May the sun always shine upon your windowpane.
May a rainbow be certain to follow each rain.
May the hand of a friend always be near to you.
And may God fill your heart with gladness
to cheer you.

—Irish Traditional

G od give us grace to accept with serenity the things
that cannot be changed, courage to change
the things that should be changed, and wisdom
to distinguish the one from the other.

—Reinhold Niebuhr

T he things, good Lord, that we pray for,
give us the grace to labour for.

—St. Thomas More

Be kind to your little children, Lord.
Be a gentle teacher, patient with our weakness and stupidity. And give us the strength and discernment to do what you tell us, and so grow in your likeness.
May we all live in the peace that comes from you.
May we journey towards your city, sailing through the waters of sin untouched by the waves, borne serenely along by the Holy Spirit.
Night and day may we give you praise and thanks, because you have shown us that all things belong to you, and all blessings are gifts from you.
To you, the essence of wisdom, the foundation of truth, be glory for evermore.

—**Clement of Alexandria**

Jesus, friend of the poor,
  Feeder of the hungry,
   Healer of the sick,
I adore thee.
…
Jesus, teacher of patience,
pattern of gentleness,
prophet of the kingdom of heaven,
I adore thee.

—*A Book of Prayers for Students,* Excerpts

Prayers and Blessings from the Bible

The Lord bless thee, and keep thee:
The Lord make his face shine upon thee,
and be gracious unto thee:
The Lord lift up his countenance upon thee,
and give thee peace.

—Numbers 6:24–26

A nd all these blessings shall come on thee,
and overtake thee,
if thou shalt hearken unto the voice of the
Lord thy God.
Blessed shalt thou be in the city,
and blessed shalt thou be in the field.
Blessed shall be the fruit of thy body,
and the fruit of thy ground,
and the fruit of thy cattle,
the increase of thy kine,
and the flocks of thy sheep.
Blessed shall be thy basket and thy store.
Blessed shalt thou be when thou comest in,
and blessed shalt thou be when thou goest out.

—**Deuteronomy 28:2–6**

Blessed are the poor in spirit:
for theirs is the kingdom of heaven.
Blessed are they that mourn:
for they shall be comforted.
Blessed are the meek: for they shall inherit the earth.
Blessed are they which do hunger and thirst after
righteousness: for they shall be filled.
Blessed are the merciful: for they shall obtain mercy.
Blessed are the pure in heart: for they shall see God.
Blessed are the peacemakers: for they shall be called
the children of God.
Blessed are they which are persecuted
for righteousness' sake:
for theirs is the kingdom of heaven.
Blessed are ye, when men shall revile you,
and persecute you, and shall say all manner of evil
against you falsely, for my sake.
Rejoice, and be exceeding glad: for great is your
reward in heaven: for so persecuted they the prophets
which were before you.

—Matthew 5:3–12

G race be unto you, and peace, from God our Father, and from the Lord Jesus Christ.

—1 Corinthians 1:3

N ow the God of hope fill you with all joy and peace in believing, that ye may abound in hope, through the power of the Holy Ghost.

—Romans 15:13

For this cause I bow my knees unto the Father of our Lord Jesus Christ, Of whom the whole family in heaven and earth is named, That he would grant you, according to the riches of his glory, to be strengthened with might by his Spirit in the inner man; That Christ may dwell in your hearts by faith; that ye, being rooted and grounded in love, May be able to comprehend with all saints what is the breadth, and length, and depth, and height; And to know the love of Christ, which passeth knowledge, that ye might be filled with all the fulness of God.

—Ephesians 3:14–19

For this cause we also, since the day we heard it, do not cease to pray for you, and to desire that ye might be filled with the knowledge of his will in all wisdom and spiritual understanding;
That ye might walk worthy of the Lord unto all pleasing, being fruitful in every good work, and increasing in the knowledge of God;
Strengthened with all might, according to his glorious power, unto all patience and longsuffering with joyfulness;
Giving thanks unto the Father, which hath made us meet to be partakers of the inheritance of the saints in light.

—Colossians 1:9–12

Prayers and Blessings for Special Occasions

God is present at our milestone moments—birthdays, weddings and anniversaries, housewarmings, and births. We know that he wants to pour blessings on us during those special times. What a gift!

For Birthdays

May you live all the days of your life.

—**Jonathan Swift**

May God grant you many years to live,
For surely he must be knowing
The earth has angels all too few
And heaven's overflowing!

—**Traditional Irish**

God grant you many and happy years,
Till when the last has crowned you
The dawn of endless day appears,
And heaven is shining round you!

—**Oliver Wendell Holmes**

For Engagements, Weddings, and Anniversaries

May all your troubles be little ones, and may you both live in love and happiness for all the days of your lives.

—**Traditional Irish**

Here's to loving, to romance, to us.
May we travel together through time.
We alone count as none, but together we're one,
For our partnership puts love to rhyme.

—**Traditional Irish**

May the flower of love never be nipped by the frost of disappointment, nor the shadow of grief fall upon you.

—Traditional Irish

Let all thy joys be as the month of May,
And all thy days be as a marriage day:
Let sorrow, sickness, and a troubled mind
Be stranger to thee.

—Francis Quarles

May you be poor in misfortune, rich in blessings, slow to make enemies, quick to make friends. But rich or poor, quick or slow, may you know nothing but happiness from this day forward.

—Traditional Irish

For Babies and Children

Where Did You Come From?

Where did you come from, baby dear?
Out of the everywhere into here.
Where did you get your eyes so blue?
Out of the sky as I came Through.
What makes the light in them sparkle and spin?
Some of the starry spikes left in.
Where did you get that little tear?
I found it waiting when I got here.

What makes your forehead so smooth and high?
A soft hand stroked it as I went by.
What makes your cheek like a warm white rose?
I saw something better than anyone knows.
Whence that three-corner'd smile of bliss?
Three angels gave me at once a kiss.
Where did you get this pearly ear?
God spoke, and it came out to hear.
Where did you get those arms and hands?
Love made itself into hooks and bands.
Whence did you come, you darling things?
From the same box as the cherubs' wings.
Where did you get that dimple so cute?
God touched my cheek as I came through.
How did they all just come to be you?
God thought of me, and so I grew.
But how did you come to us, you dear?
God thought of you, and so I am here.

—George MacDonald

A Cradle Hymn

Hush, my dear, lie still and slumber,
Holy angels guard thy bed!
Heavenly blessings without number
Gently falling on thy head.
How much better thou'rt attended
Than the Son of God could be
When from heaven he descended,
And became a child like thee.

—Isaac Watts

For Travelers

May the road rise to meet you.
May the wind be always at your back.
May the sun shine warm upon your face;
The rains fall soft upon your fields
And, until we meet again,
May God hold you in the palm of His hand.

—**Traditional Irish**

For the Home

May your troubles be less and your blessings be more and nothing but happiness come through your door.

—**Traditional Irish**

Bless our homes, dear God, that we cherish the daily bread before there is none, discover each other before we leave on our separate ways, and enjoy each other for what we are, while we have time to do so.

—**Hawaiian (adapted)**

May the winds of adversity ne'er blow open our door.

—**Scottish Blessing**

Home Song

I read within
a poet's book
A word that
starred the
page, "Stone
walls do not a
prison make,
Nor iron bars
a cage."
Yes, that is true,
and something
more:
You'll find,
where'er
you roam,
That marble floors and gilded walls
Can never make a home.
But every house where Love abides
And Friendship is a guest,
Is surely home, and home, sweet home;
For there the heart can rest.

—Henry Van Dyke

L ord, behold our family here assembled. We thank you this place in which we dwell, for the love that unites us, for the peace accorded us this day, for the hope with which we expect the morrow; for the health, the work, the food and the bright skies that make our lives delightful; for our friends in all parts of the earth. Amen.

—Robert Louis Stevenson

M ay the roof above us never fall in, and may we friends gathered below never fall out.

—Traditional Irish

God bless the corners of this house,
and be the lintel blessed,
And bless the hearth,
And bless the board,
And bless each place of rest.
Bless each door that opens wide to
strangers and to kin,
And bless each crystal windowpane,
that lets the sunshine in.
And bless the rooftree overhead,
And every sturdy wall,
The peace of man,
The peace of God,
The peace of love to all.

—**Traditional Irish**

Praise and Thanksgiving

When we read the Bible, we see wonderful examples of prayers of praise and thanksgiving. In fact, without praise, the soul withers. Even when you feel overwhelmed or in need of help, it is good to take the time to thank God and to praise him for all he is and all he does for us.

We Gather Together

We gather together to ask the Lord's blessing;
he chastens and hastens his will
to make known;
the wicked oppressing now cease from distressing.
Sing praises to his name; he forgets not his own.

Beside us to guide us, our God with us joining,
ordaining, maintaining his kingdom divine;
so from the beginning the fight we were winning;
thou, Lord, wast at our side; all glory be thine!

We all do extol thee, thou leader triumphant,
and pray that thou still our defender wilt be.
Let thy congregation escape tribulation;
thy name be ever praised! O Lord, make us free!

—Netherlands traditional, trans. Theodore Baker

All Hail the Power of Jesus' Name

All hail the power of Jesus' name!
Let angels prostrate fall.
Bring forth the royal diadem,
and crown him Lord of all.
Bring forth the royal diadem,
and crown him Lord of all!

O seed of Israel's chosen race
now ransomed from the fall,
hail him who saves you by his grace,

and crown him Lord of all.
Hail him who saves you by his grace,
and crown him
Lord of all!

Let every tongue
and every tribe
responsive to
his call,
to him all
majesty ascribe,
and crown him
Lord of all.
To him all
majesty ascribe,
and crown him
Lord of all!

Oh, that with all the sacred throng
we at his feet may fall!
We'll join the everlasting song
and crown him Lord of all.
We'll join the everlasting song
and crown him Lord of all.

—Edward Perronet

For the Beauty of the Earth

For the beauty of the earth,
for the glory of the skies,
for the love which from our birth
over and around us lies.
Christ, our Lord, to you we raise
this, our hymn of grateful praise.

For the wonder of each hour
of the day and of the night,
hill and vale and tree and flower,
sun and moon and stars of light,

Christ, our Lord, to you we raise
this, our hymn of grateful praise.

For the joy of human love,
brother, sister, parent, child,
friends on earth, and friends above,
for all gentle thoughts and mild,
Christ, our Lord, to you we raise this,
our hymn of
grateful praise.

For yourself,
best gift divine,
to the world so
freely given,
agent of God's
grand design:
peace on earth
and joy
in heaven.
Christ, our
Lord, to you
we raise this,
our hymn of grateful praise.

—Folliott S. Pierpont

Holy, Holy, Holy! Lord God Almighty

Holy, holy, holy! Lord God Almighty!
Early in the morning our song shall rise to thee;
holy, holy, holy! merciful and mighty,
God in three persons, blessed Trinity!

Holy, holy, holy! All the saints adore thee,
casting down their golden crowns around
the glassy sea;
cherubim and seraphim falling down before thee,
who wert and art and evermore shalt be.

Holy, holy, holy! Though the darkness hide thee,
though the eye made blind by sin thy glory
may not see,
only thou art holy; there is none beside thee,
perfect in power, in love, and purity.

Holy, holy, holy! Lord God Almighty!
All thy works shall praise thy name,
in earth and sky and sea;
holy, holy, holy! merciful and mighty,
God in three persons, blessed Trinity!

—Reginald Heber

All praise to Him who now hath turned
My fears to joys, my sighs to song,
My tears to smiles, my sad to glad. Amen.

—**Anne Bradstreet**

Christ, the Lord, is risen today,
Sons of God and angels say,
Raise your joys and triumphs high,
Sing, ye heavens, and earth rely.

—**Charles Wesley**

If my lips could sing as many songs as there are waves in the sea:
if my tongue could sing as many hymns as there are ocean billows:
if my mouth filled the whole firmament with praise:
if my faith shone like the sun and moon together:
if my hands were to hover in the sky like powerful eagles and my feet ran across mountains as swiftly as the deer;
all that would not be enough to pay you fitting tribute, O Lord my God.

—Jewish Prayer

Count Your Blessings

When upon life's billows you are tempest tossed,
When you are discouraged, thinking all is lost,
Count your many blessings, name them one by one,
And it will surprise you what the Lord hath done.

Count your blessings, name them one by one:
Count your blessings, see what God hath done.
Count your blessings, name them one by one;
Count your many blessings, see what God
hath done.

—Johnson Oatman, Jr.

O Word of God Incarnate

O Word of God Incarnate,
O Wisdom from on high,
O Truth unchanged, unchanging,
O Light of our dark sky:
We praise thee for the radiance
That from the hallowed page,
A lantern to our footsteps,
Shines on from age to age.

—William Walsham How

Blessed and praised be the Lord, from whom comes all the good that we speak and think and do.

—**Teresa of Avila**

Thou who has given so much to me,
give me one thing more: a grateful heart.

—**George Herbert**

If the only prayer you say in your entire life
is Thank you, that would suffice.

—**Meister Eckhart**

Blessed Assurance

Blessed assurance, Jesus is mine!
Oh what a foretaste of glory divine!
Heir of salvation, purchase of God,
Born of His Spirit, washed in His blood.
Perfect submission, perfect delight!
Visions of rapture now burst on my sight;
Angels descending bring from above
Echoes of mercy, whispers of love.
Perfect submission—all is at rest,
I in my Savior am happy and blest;
Watching and waiting, looking above,
Filled with His goodness, lost in His love.
This is my story, this is my song,
Praising my Savior all the day long;
This is my story, this is my song,
Praising my Savior all the day long.

—Fanny J. Crosby

We Plow the Fields and Scatter

We plow the fields and scatter
The good seed on the land,
But it is fed and watered
By God's almighty hand;
He sends the snow in winter,
The warmth to swell the grain,
The breezes and the sunshine,
And soft, refreshing rain.

All good gifts around us
Are sent from heaven above:
Then thank the Lord,
O thank the Lord
For all His love.

—Matthias Claudius

Thou, my all! My theme!
My inspiration! and my crown!
My strength in age—my rise in low estate!
My soul's ambition, pleasure, wealth!—my world!
My light in darkness!
and my life in death!
My boast through time! bliss through eternity!
Eternity too short to speak thy praise!
Or fathom thy profound love to man!

—**Edward Young**

H oly Spirit, the life that gives life.
You are the cause of all movement;
You are the breath of all creatures;
You are the salve that purifies our souls;
You are the ointment that heals our wounds;
You are the fire that warms our hearts;
You are the light that guides our feet.
Let all the world praise you.

—**Hildegard of Bingen**

On Our Way Rejoicing

On our way to rejoicing gladly let us go.
Christ our Lord has conquered;
vanquished is the foe.
Christ without, our safety;
Christ within, our joy;
who, if we be faithful,
can our hope destroy?
On our way rejoicing;
as we forward move,
hearken to our praises,
O lest God of love!

Unto God the Father joyful songs we sing;
unto God the Savior thankful hearts we bring;
unto God the Spirit bow we and adore,
on our way rejoicing now and evermore.
On our way rejoicing;
as we forward move,
hearken to our praises,
O blest God of love!

—John S. Monsell

Praise to the Lord, the Almighty

Praise to the Lord, the Almighty, the King of creation! O my soul, praise him, for he is your health and salvation! Come, all who hear; now to his temple draw near, join me in glad adoration.

Praise to the Lord, above all things so wondrously reigning; sheltering you under his wings, and so gently sustaining! Have you not seen all that is needful has been sent by his gracious ordaining?

Praise to the Lord, who will prosper your work and defend you; surely his goodness and mercy shall daily attend you. Ponder anew what the Almighty can do, if with his love he befriends you.

Praise to the Lord! O let all that is in me adore him! All that has life and breath, come now with praises before him. Let the Amen sound from his people again; gladly forever adore him.

—Joachim Neander, trans. Catherine Winkworth

Now Thank We All Our God

Now thank we all our God
with hearts and hands and voices,
who wondrous things hath done,
in whom this world rejoices;
who, from our mothers' arms,
hath blessed us on our way
with countless gifts of love,
and still is ours today.

—Martin Rinkart, trans. Catherine Winkworth

Thanksgiving is nothing if not a glad and reverent
lifting of the heart to God in honour and praise
for His goodness.

—James R. Miller

The Song of Moses

Then sang Moses and the children of Israel this song unto the Lord, and spake, saying, I will sing unto the Lord, for he hath triumphed gloriously: the horse and his rider hath he thrown into the sea.

The Lord is my strength and song, and he is become my salvation: he is my God, and I will prepare him an habitation; my father's God, and I will exalt him. The Lord is a man of war: the Lord is his name.

Pharaoh's chariots and his host hath he cast into the sea: his chosen captains also are drowned in the Red sea.

The depths have covered them: they sank into the bottom as a stone.

Thy right hand, O Lord, is become glorious in power: thy right hand, O Lord, hath dashed in pieces the enemy.

And in the greatness of thine excellency thou hast overthrown them that rose up against thee: thou sentest forth thy wrath, which consumed them as stubble.

And with the blast of thy nostrils the waters were gathered together, the floods stood upright as an heap, and the depths were congealed in the heart of the sea.

The enemy said, I will pursue, I will overtake, I will divide the spoil; my lust shall be satisfied upon them; will draw my sword, my hand shall destroy them.

Thou didst blow with thy wind, the sea covered them: they sank as lead in the mighty waters.

Who is like unto thee, O Lord, among the gods? Who is like thee, glorious in holiness, fearful in praises, doing wonders? Thou stretchedst out thy right hand, the earth swallowed them.

Thou in thy mercy hast led forth the people which thou hast redeemed: thou hast guided them in thy strength unto thy holy habitation.

The people shall hear, and be afraid: sorrow shall take
hold on the inhabitants of Palestina.

Then the dukes of Edom shall be amazed; the mighty
men of Moab, trembling shall take hold upon them;
all the inhabitants of Canaan shall melt away.

Fear and dread shall fall upon them; by the greatness
of thine arm they shall be as still as a stone;
till thy people pass over, O Lord, till the people
pass over, which thou hast purchased.

Thou shalt bring them in, and plant them in the
mountain of thine inheritance, in the place,
O Lord, which thou hast made for thee to dwell in,
in the Sanctuary, O Lord, which thy hands
have established.

The Lord shall reign for ever and ever.

—Exodus 15:1–18

A Prayer of Moses

Give ear, O ye heavens, and I will speak;
and hear, O earth, the words of my mouth.
My doctrine shall drop as the rain, my speech shall
distil as the dew, as the small rain upon the tender
herb, and as the showers upon the grass:
Because I will publish the name of the Lord:
ascribe ye greatness unto our God.
He is the Rock, his work is perfect: for all his ways
are judgment: a God of truth and without iniquity,
just and right is he.

—Deuteronomy 32:1–4

Hannah's Prayer

And Hannah prayed, and said, My heart rejoiceth in the Lord, mine horn is exalted in the Lord: my mouth is enlarged over mine enemies; because I rejoice in thy salvation.
There is none holy as the Lord: for there is none beside thee: neither is there any rock like our God.
Talk no more so exceeding proudly; let not arrogancy come out of your mouth: for the Lord is a God of knowledge, and by him actions are weighed.

The bows of the mighty men are broken, and they that stumbled are girded with strength.
They that were full have hired out themselves for bread; and they that were hungry ceased: so that the barren hath born seven; and she that hath many children is waxed feeble.

The Lord killeth, and maketh alive:
he bringeth down to the grave, and bringeth up.
The Lord maketh poor, and maketh rich:
he bringeth low, and lifteth up.
He raiseth up the poor out of the dust, and lifteth up
the beggar from the dunghill, to set them among
princes, and to make them inherit the throne of glory:
for the pillars of the earth are the Lord's, and he hath
set the world upon them.
He will keep the feet of his saints, and the wicked
shall be silent in darkness; for by strength shall
no man prevail.
The adversaries of the Lord shall be broken to pieces;
out of heaven shall he thunder upon them: the Lord
shall judge the ends of the earth; and he shall give
strength unto his king, and exalt the horn of
his anointed.

—1 Samuel 2:1–10

Psalm 8

O Lord, our Lord, how excellent is thy name in
all the earth! who hast set thy glory above
the heavens.
Out of the mouth of babes and sucklings hast
thou ordained strength because of thine enemies,
that thou mightest still the enemy and the avenger.
When I consider thy heavens, the work of thy fingers,
the moon and the stars, which thou hast ordained;
What is man, that thou art mindful of him? and the
son of man, that thou visitest him?
For thou hast made him a little lower than the angels,
and hast crowned him with glory and honour.
Thou madest him to have dominion over the works
of thy hands; thou hast put all things under his feet:
All sheep and oxen, yea, and the beasts of the field;
The fowl of the air, and the fish of the sea,
and whatsoever passeth through the paths of the seas.
O Lord our Lord, how excellent is thy name in
all the earth!

Psalm 19

The heavens declare the glory of God; and the firmament sheweth his handywork.

Day unto day uttereth speech, and night unto night sheweth knowledge.

There is no speech nor language, where their voice is not heard.

Their line is gone out through all the earth, and their words to the end of the world. In them hath he set a tabernacle for the sun,

Which is as a bridegroom coming out of his chamber,

and rejoiceth as a strong man to run a race.
His going forth is from the end of the heaven,
and his circuit unto the ends of it: and there is nothing
hid from the heat thereof.
The law of the Lord is perfect, converting the soul: the
testimony of the Lord is sure, making wise the simple.
The statutes of the Lord are right, rejoicing the heart:
the commandment of the Lord is pure,
enlightening the eyes.
The fear of the Lord is clean, enduring for ever:
the judgments of the Lord are true and righteous
altogether.
More to be desired are they than gold, yea, than much
fine gold: sweeter also than honey and the honeycomb.
Moreover by them is thy servant warned: and in
keeping of them there is great reward.
Who can understand his errors? cleanse thou me from
secret faults.
Keep back thy servant also from presumptuous sins;
let them not have dominion over me: then shall I be
upright, and I shall be innocent from the great
transgression.
Let the words of my mouth, and the meditation of my
heart, be acceptable in thy sight, O Lord, my strength,
and my redeemer.

Psalm 67

God be merciful unto us, and bless us;
and cause his face to shine upon us; Selah.
That thy way may be known upon earth,
thy saving health among all nations.
Let the people praise thee, O God; let all the
people praise thee.
O let the nations be glad and sing for joy:
for thou shalt judge the people righteously,
and govern the nations upon earth. Selah.
Let the people praise thee, O God;
let all the people praise thee.
Then shall the earth yield her increase;
and God, even our own God, shall bless us.
God shall bless us; and all the ends of the
earth shall fear him.

Psalm 95

O come, let us sing unto the Lord: let us make a joyful noise to the rock of our salvation.
Let us come before his presence with thanksgiving, and make a joyful noise unto him with psalms.
For the Lord is a great God, and a great King above all gods.
In his hand are the deep places of the earth: the strength of the hills is his also.
The sea is his, and he made it: and his hands formed the dry land.
O come, let us
worship and bow down: let us kneel before the Lord our maker.
For he is our God; and we are the people of his pasture, and the sheep of his hand. To day if ye will hear his voice,
Harden not your heart, as in the provocation,

and as in the day of temptation in the wilderness:
When your fathers tempted me, proved me,
and saw my work.
Forty years long was I grieved with this generation,
and said, It is a people that do err in their heart,
and they have not known my ways:
Unto whom I sware in my wrath that they should
not enter into my rest.

Psalm 98

O sing unto the Lord a new song; for he hath done marvellous things: his right hand, and his holy arm, hath gotten him the victory.
The Lord hath made known his salvation:
his righteousness hath he openly shewed in
the sight of the heathen.
He hath remembered his mercy and his truth toward the house of Israel: all the ends of the earth have seen the salvation of our God.

Make a joyful noise unto the Lord, all the earth:
make a loud noise, and rejoice, and sing praise.
Sing unto the Lord with the harp; with the harp,
and the voice of a psalm.
With trumpets and sound of cornet make a joyful noise
before the Lord, the King.
Let the sea roar, and the fulness thereof;
the world, and they that dwell therein.
Let the floods clap their hands:
let the hills be joyful together
Before the Lord; for he cometh to judge the earth:
with righteousness shall he judge the world,
and the people with equity.

Psalm 100

Make a joyful noise unto the Lord, all ye lands. Serve the Lord with gladness: come before his presence with singing.
Know ye that the Lord he is God: it is he that hath made us, and not we ourselves; we are his people, and the sheep of his pasture.  Enter into his gates with thanksgiving, and into his courts with praise: be thankful unto him, and bless his name.
For the Lord is good; his mercy is everlasting; and his truth endureth to all generations.

Psalm 113

Praise ye the Lord. Praise, O ye servants of the Lord, praise the name of the Lord.

Blessed be the name of the Lord from this time forth and for evermore.

From the rising of the sun unto the going down of the same the Lord's name is to be praised.

The Lord is high above all nations, and his glory above the heavens.

Who is like unto the Lord our God, who dwelleth on high,

Who humbleth himself to behold the things that are in heaven, and in the earth!

He raiseth up the poor out of the dust, and lifteth the needy out of the dunghill;

That he may set him with princes, even with the princes of his people.

He maketh the barren woman to keep house, and to be a joyful mother of children. Praise ye the Lord.

Psalm 150

Praise ye the Lord.
Praise God in his sanctuary:
praise him in the firmament of his power.
Praise him for his mighty acts:
praise him according to his excellent greatness.
Praise him with the sound of the trumpet:
praise him with the psaltery and harp.
Praise him with the timbrel and dance:
praise him with stringed instruments and organs.
Praise him upon the loud cymbals:
praise him upon the high sounding cymbals.
Let every thing that hath breath praise the Lord.
Praise ye the Lord.

Daniel's Prayer

Daniel answered and said, Blessed be the name of God for ever and ever: for wisdom and might are his:
And he changeth the times and the seasons: he removeth kings, and setteth up kings: he giveth wisdom unto the wise, and knowledge to them that know understanding:
He revealeth the deep and secret things: he knoweth what is in the darkness, and the light dwelleth with him.
I thank thee, and praise thee, O thou God of my fathers, who hast given me wisdom and might, and hast made known unto me now what we desired of thee.

—Daniel 2:20-23

Mary's Prayer

And Mary said, My soul doth magnify the Lord, And my spirit hath rejoiced in God my Saviour.
For he hath regarded the low estate of his hand-maiden: for, behold, from henceforth all generations shall call me blessed.
For he that is mighty hath done to me great things; and holy is his name.
And his mercy is on them that fear him from generation to generation.
He hath shewed strength with his arm; he hath scattered the proud in the imagination of their hearts.
He hath put down the mighty from their seats, and exalted them of low degree.
He hath filled the hungry with good things; and the rich he hath sent empty away.
He hath helped his servant Israel, in remembrance of his mercy;
As he spake to our fathers, to Abraham, and to his seed for ever.

—Luke 1:46-55

Zechariah's Prayer

B lessed be the Lord God of Israel;
for he hath visited and redeemed his people,
And hath raised up an horn of salvation for us
in the house of his servant David;
As he spake by the mouth of his holy prophets,
which have been since the world began:
That we should be saved from our enemies,
and from the hand of all that hate us;
To perform the mercy promised to our fathers,

and to remember his holy covenant;
The oath which he sware to our father Abraham,
That he would grant unto us, that we being delivered
out of the hand of our enemies might serve him
without fear,
In holiness and righteousness before him,
all the days of our life.
And thou, child, shalt be called the prophet of the
Highest: for thou shalt go before the face of the
Lord to prepare his ways;
To give knowledge of salvation unto his people by the
remission of their sins,
Through the tender mercy of our God;
whereby the dayspring from on high hath visited us,
To give light to them that sit in darkness and in the
shadow of death, to guide our feet into the way
of peace.

—Luke 1:68-79

And the multitudes that went before, and that followed, cried, saying, Hosanna to the son of David: Blessed is he that cometh in the name of the Lord; Hosanna in the highest.

—Matthew 21:9

Glory to God in the highest, and on earth peace, good will toward men.

—Luke 2:14

God's Creation

We see God's hand in nature, in all the wonderful world around us. How beautiful God's work is! Let us take the time to appreciate it and express our appreciation to our Creator God.

Joyful, Joyful, We Adore Thee

Joyful, joyful, we adore thee,
    God of glory, Lord of love;
hearts unfold like flow'rs before thee,
op'ning to the sun above.
Melt the clouds of sin and sadness,
drive the dark of doubt away;
giver of immortal gladness,
fill us with the light of day.
All thy works with joy surround thee,
earth and heav'n reflect thy rays,
stars and angels sing around thee,
center of unbroken praise.
Field and forest, vale and mountain,
flowery meadow, flashing sea,
chanting bird and flowing fountain,
call us to rejoice in thee.

—Henry van Dyke

The Canticle of Brother Sun

Praised be You, my Lord, through our Sister Mother
Earth, who sustains us, governs us, and who
produces varied fruits with coloured flowers and herbs.
Praised be You, my Lord, through Brother Wind and
through the air, cloudy and serene, and every kind
of weather.
Praised be You, my Lord, through Sister Moon and the
stars in heaven: you formed them clear and precious
and beautiful.
Praised be You, my Lord, through Brother Fire,
through whom You light the night and he is
beautiful and playful and robust and strong.
Praised be You, my Lord, with all your creatures,
especially Sir Brother Sun, who is the day and
through whom you give us light. And he is
beautiful and radiant with great splendours
and bears likeness of You, Most High One.

—St. Francis of Assisi

How Great Thou Art

OLord my God! When I in awesome wonder
Consider all the works Thy hand hath made.
I see the stars, I hear the rolling thunder,
Thy power throughout the universe displayed.

Then sings my soul, my Saviour God, to Thee;
How great Thou art, how great Thou art!
Then sings my soul, my Saviour God, to Thee:
How great Thou art, how great Thou art!

When through the woods and forest glades I wander
And hear the birds sing sweetly in the trees;
When I look down from lofty mountain grandeur
And hear the brook and feel the gentle breeze:

Then sings my soul, my Saviour God, to Thee;
How great Thou art, how great Thou art!
Then sings my soul, my Saviour God, to Thee:
How great Thou art, how great Thou art!

And when I think that God, His Son not sparing,
Sent Him to die, I scarce can take it in;
That on the cross, my burden gladly bearing,
He bled and died to take away my sin:

Then sings my soul, my Saviour God, to Thee;
How great Thou art, how great Thou art!
Then sings my soul, my Saviour God, to Thee:
How great Thou art, how great Thou art!

When Christ shall come with shout of acclamation
And take me home, what joy shall fill my heart!
Then I shall bow in humble adoration,
And there proclaim, my God, how great Thou art!

—Carl Gustav Boberg

All Creatures of Our God and King

All creatures of our God and King,
lift up your voice and with us sing:
alleluia, alleluia!
O burning
sun with
golden beam,
and shining
moon with
silver gleam,
O praise him,
O praise him,
alleluia,
alleluia,
alleluia!
O rushing wind
so wild and
strong,
white clouds
that sail in
heaven along,
alleluia, alleluia!
New rising dawn in praise rejoice;
you lights of evening find a voice:
O praise him, O praise him,
alleluia, alleluia, alleluia!

Cool flowing water, pure and clear,
make music for your Lord to hear:
alleluia, alleluia!
Fierce fire, so masterful and bright,
providing us with warmth and light.
O praise him, O praise him,
alleluia, alleluia, alleluia!
Earth ever fertile, day by day
bring forth your blessings on our way;
alleluia, alleluia!
All flowers and fruits that in you grow,
let them his glory also show;
O praise him, O praise him,
alleluia, alleluia, alleluia!
All you who are of tender heart,
forgiving others, take your part;
alleluia, alleluia!
All you who pain and sorrow bear,
praise God and on him cast your care;
O praise him, O praise him,
alleluia, alleluia, alleluia!
Let all things their Creator bless,
and worship him in humbleness,
alleluia, alleluia!
Praise, praise the Father, praise the Son,
and praise the Spirit, Three in One:
O praise him, O praise him,
alleluia, alleluia, alleluia!

—St. Francis of Assisi

God's Grandeur

The world is charged with the grandeur of God.
　It will flame out, like shining from shook foil;
It gathers to a greatness, like the ooze of oil
Crushed. Why do men then now not reck his rod?
Generations have trod, have trod, have trod;
And all is seared with trade; bleared, smeared with toil;
And wears man's smudge and shares man's smell:
the soil
Is bare now, nor can foot feel, being shod.
And for all this, nature is never spent;
There lives the dearest freshness deep down things;
And though the last lights off the black West went
Oh, morning, at the brown brink eastward, springs—
Because the Holy Ghost over the bent
World broods with warm breast
and with ah! bright wings.

—Gerard Manley Hopkins

When I first open my eyes upon the morning meadows and look out upon the beautiful world, I thank God I am alive.

—Ralph Waldo Emerson

God passes through the thicket of the world, and wherever his glance falls he turns all things to beauty.

—St. John of the Cross

Glory be to God for dappled things— For skies as couple-color as a brinded cow; For rose-moles all in stipple upon trout that swim.

—Gerard Manley Hopkins

Psalm 29

Give unto the Lord, O ye mighty, give unto the Lord glory and strength.
Give unto the Lord the glory due unto his name;
worship the Lord in the beauty of holiness.
The voice of the Lord is upon the waters:
the God of glory thundereth:
the Lord is upon many waters.
The voice of the Lord is powerful;
the voice of the Lord is full of majesty.
The voice of the Lord breaketh the cedars;
yea, the Lord breaketh the cedars of Lebanon.
He maketh them also to skip like a calf;
Lebanon and Sirion like a young unicorn.
The voice of the Lord divideth the flames of fire.
The voice of the Lord shaketh the wilderness;
the Lord shaketh the wilderness of Kadesh.
The voice of the Lord maketh the hinds to calve,
and discovereth the forests:
and in his temple doth every one speak of his glory.
The Lord sitteth upon the flood;
yea, the Lord sitteth King for ever.
The Lord will give strength unto his people;
the Lord will bless his people with peace.

Psalm 93

The Lord reigneth, he is clothed with majesty; the Lord is clothed with strength, wherewith he hath girded himself: the world also is stablished, that it cannot be moved.
Thy throne is established of old: thou art from everlasting.
The floods have lifted up, O Lord, the floods have lifted up their voice; the floods lift up their waves.
The Lord on high is mightier than the noise of many waters, yea, than the mighty waves of the sea.
Thy testimonies are very sure: holiness becometh thine house, O Lord, for ever.

Psalm 148

Praise ye the Lord.
  Praise ye the Lord from the heavens:
praise him in the heights.
Praise ye him, all his angels:
praise ye him, all his hosts.
Praise ye him, sun and moon:
praise him, all ye stars of light.

Praise him, ye heavens of heavens,
and ye waters that be above the heavens.

Let them praise the name of the Lord:
for he commanded, and they were created.
He hath also stablished them for ever and ever:
he hath made a decree which shall not pass.
Praise the Lord from the earth,
ye dragons, and all deeps:
Fire, and hail; snow, and vapours;
stormy wind fulfilling his word:
Mountains, and all hills; fruitful trees, and all cedars:
Beasts, and all cattle; creeping things, and flying fowl:
Kings of the earth, and all people;
princes, and all judges of the earth:
Both young men, and maidens; old men, and children:
Let them praise the name of the Lord:
for his name alone is excellent;
his glory is above the earth and heaven.
He also exalteth the horn of his people,
the praise of all his saints; even of the children
of Israel, a people near unto him. Praise ye the Lord.

Repentance and Forgiveness

Love and forgiveness walk hand-in-hand. Our relationships with God and others are intertwined in this dynamic. We need God's mercy, and we need to extend that mercy to others when they hurt us. Sometimes finding the words to ask for forgiveness can be difficult; this section includes prayers and hymns to help give us words.

Forgive

If I have wounded any soul today,
If I have caused one foot to go astray,
If I have walked in my own willful way,
Dear Lord, forgive!
If I have uttered idle words or vain,
If I have turned aside from want or pain,
Lest I myself shall suffer through the strain,
Dear Lord, forgive!
Forgive the sins I have confessed to Thee;
Forgive the secret sins I do not see;
O guide me, love me and my keeper be,
Dear Lord, Amen.

—C. Maude Battersby

D ear Lord and Father of humankind,
   Forgive our foolish ways;
Reclothe us in our rightful mind,
In purer lives Thy service find,
In deeper reverence, praise.

—John Greenleaf Whittier

The Lord hath spoken peace to my soul,
He hath blessed me abundantly,
Hath pardoned my sins;
He hath shown me great mercy and
saved me by his love.
I will sing of his goodness and mercy while I live,
And ever, forever will praise his holy name.
O how sweet to trust in God,
And to know your sins forgiven,
To believe his precious word,
And be guided by his love.
Therefore goodness and mercy,
Shall follow me all the days of my life.
Amen.

—C.E. Leslie

Lord, I Confess to Thee

Lord, I confess to you,
sadly, my sin;
all I am, I tell to you,
all I have been.
Purge all my sin away,
wash clean my soul
this day;
Lord, make me clean.
Then all is peace and
light this soul within;
thus shall I walk with you,
loved though unseen.
Leaning on you, my God,
guided along the road,
nothing between!

—Horatius Bonar

A Prayer of Moses

And Moses made haste, and bowed his head toward the earth, and worshipped. And he said, If now I have found grace in thy sight, O Lord, let my Lord, I pray thee, go among us; for it is a stiffnecked people; and pardon our iniquity and our sin, and take us for thine inheritance.

—Exodus 34:8–9

A Prayer of Daniel

And I prayed unto the Lord my God, and made my confession, and said, O Lord, the great and dreadful God, keeping the covenant and mercy to them that love him, and to them that keep his commandments;
We have sinned, and have committed iniquity, and have done wickedly, and have rebelled, even by departing from thy precepts and from thy judgments: Neither have we hearkened unto thy servants the prophets, which spake in thy name to our kings, our princes, and our fathers, and to all the people of the land.

O Lord, righteousness belongeth unto thee, but unto us confusion of faces, as at this day; to the men of Judah, and to the inhabitants of Jerusalem, and unto all Israel, that are near, and that are far off, through all the countries whither thou hast driven them, because of their trespass that they have trespassed against thee.

O Lord, to us belongeth confusion of face, to our kings, to our princes, and to our fathers, because we have sinned against thee.

To the Lord our God belong mercies and forgivenesses, though we have rebelled against him;

Neither have we obeyed the voice of the Lord our God, to walk in his laws, which he set before us by his servants the prophets. Yea, all Israel have transgressed thy law, even by departing, that they might not obey thy voice; therefore the curse is poured upon us, and the oath that is written in the law of Moses the servant of God, because we

have sinned against him.

And he hath confirmed his words, which he spake against us, and against our judges that judged us, by bringing upon us a great evil: for under the whole heaven hath not been done as hath been done upon Jerusalem.

As it is written in the law of Moses, all this evil is come upon us: yet made we not our prayer before the Lord our God, that we might turn from our iniquities, and understand thy truth.

Therefore hath the Lord watched upon the evil, and brought it upon us: for the Lord our God is righteous in all his works which he doeth: for we obeyed not his voice.

And now, O Lord our God, that hast brought thy people forth out of the land of Egypt with a mighty hand, and hast gotten thee renown, as at this day; we have sinned, we have done wickedly.

O Lord, according to all thy righteousness, I beseech thee, let thine anger and thy fury be turned away from thy city Jerusalem, thy holy mountain: because for our sins, and for the iniquities of our fathers, Jerusalem and thy people are become a reproach to all that are about us.

Now therefore, O our God, hear the prayer of thy servant, and his supplications, and cause thy face to shine upon thy sanctuary that is desolate, for the Lord's sake.

O my God, incline thine ear, and hear; open thine eyes, and behold our desolations, and the city which is called by thy name: for we do not present our supplications before thee for our righteousnesses, but for thy great mercies.

O Lord, hear; O Lord, forgive; O Lord, hearken and do; defer not, for thine own sake, O my God: for thy city and thy people are called by thy name.

—**Daniel 9:4–19**

A Prayer of Ezra

And at the evening sacrifice I arose up from my heaviness; and having rent my garment and my mantle, I fell upon my knees, and spread out my hands unto the Lord my God,
And said, O my God, I am ashamed and blush to lift up my face to thee, my God: for our iniquities are increased over our head, and our trespass is grown up unto the heavens.

—Ezra 9:5–6

A Prayer of Nehemiah

I beseech thee, O Lord God of heaven, the great and terrible God, that keepeth covenant and mercy for them that love him and observe his commandments: Let thine ear now be attentive, and thine eyes open, that thou mayest hear the prayer of thy servant, which I pray before thee now, day and night, for the children of Israel thy servants, and confess the sins of the children of Israel, which we have sinned against thee: both I and my father's house have sinned. We have dealt very corruptly against thee, and have not kept the commandments,

nor the statutes, nor the judgments,
which thou commandedst thy servant Moses.
Remember, I beseech thee, the word that thou
commandedst thy servant Moses, saying,
If ye transgress, I will scatter you abroad among the
nations: But if ye turn unto me, and keep my
commandments, and do them; though there were of
you cast out unto the uttermost part of the heaven,
yet will I gather them from thence, and will bring
them unto the place that I have chosen to set my name
there. Now these are thy servants and thy people,
whom thou hast redeemed by thy great power,
and by thy strong hand.
O Lord, I beseech thee, let now thine ear be attentive
to the prayer of thy servant, and to the prayer of thy
servants, who desire to fear thy name: and prosper,
I pray thee, thy servant this day, and grant him mercy
in the sight of this man.

—Nehemiah 1:5–11

Psalm 51

Have mercy upon me, O God, according to thy lovingkindness: according unto the multitude of thy tender mercies blot out my transgressions.
Wash me throughly from mine iniquity,
and cleanse me from my sin.
For I acknowledge my transgressions:
and my sin is ever before me.
Against thee, thee only, have I sinned, and done this evil in thy sight: that thou mightest be justified when thou speakest, and be clear when thou judgest.
Behold, I was shapen in iniquity; and in sin did my mother conceive me.
Behold, thou desirest truth in the inward parts: and in the hidden part thou shalt make me to know wisdom.
Purge me with hyssop, and I shall be clean: wash me, and I shall be whiter than snow.
Make me to hear joy and gladness; that the bones which thou hast broken may rejoice.
Hide thy face from my sins,
and blot out all mine iniquities.
Create in me a clean heart, O God;
and renew a right spirit within me.
Cast me not away from thy presence;
and take not thy holy spirit from me.
Restore unto me the joy of thy salvation;

and uphold me with thy free spirit.
Then will I teach transgressors thy ways;
and sinners shall be converted unto thee.
Deliver me from bloodguiltiness, O God, thou God
of my salvation: and my tongue shall sing aloud
of thy righteousness.
O Lord, open thou my lips; and my mouth shall
shew forth thy praise.
For thou desirest not sacrifice; else would I give it: thou
delightest not in burnt offering.
The sacrifices of God are a broken spirit: a broken
and a contrite heart, O God, thou wilt not despise.
Do good in thy good pleasure unto Zion:
build thou the walls of Jerusalem.
Then shalt thou be pleased with the sacrifices
of righteousness, with burnt offering and whole burnt
offering: then shall they offer bullocks upon thine altar.

Psalm 103

Bless the Lord, O my soul:
and all that is within me,
bless his holy name.
Bless the Lord, O my soul,
and forget not all his benefits:
Who forgiveth all thine iniquities;
who healeth all thy diseases;
Who redeemeth thy life from destruction;
who crowneth thee with lovingkindness
and tender mercies;
Who satisfieth thy mouth with good things;
so that thy youth is renewed like the eagle's.
The Lord executeth righteousness and judgment
for all that are oppressed.
He made known his ways unto Moses,
his acts unto the children of Israel.
The Lord is merciful and gracious,
slow to anger, and plenteous in mercy.
He will not always chide: neither will he
keep his anger for ever.
He hath not dealt with us after our sins;
nor rewarded us according to our iniquities.
For as the heaven is high above the earth,
so great is his mercy toward them that fear him.
As far as the east is from the west,

so far hath he removed our transgressions from us.
Like as a father pitieth his children,
so the Lord pitieth them that fear him.
For he knoweth our frame;
he remembereth that we are dust.
As for man, his days are as grass:
as a flower of the field, so he flourisheth.
For the wind passeth over it, and it is gone;
and the place thereof shall know it no more.

But the mercy of the Lord is from everlasting
to everlasting upon them that fear him,
and his righteousness unto children's children;
To such as keep his covenant, and to those that
remember his commandments to do them.
The Lord hath prepared his throne in the heavens;
and his kingdom ruleth over all.

Bless the Lord, ye his angels,
that excel in strength,
that do his commandments,
hearkening unto the voice of his word.
Bless ye the Lord, all ye his hosts;
ye ministers of his, that do his pleasure.
Bless the Lord, all his works in all places
of his dominion: bless the Lord, O my soul.

Come, and let us return unto the Lord:
for he hath torn, and he will heal us;
he hath smitten, and he will bind us up.
After two days will he revive us: in the third day he
will raise us up, and we shall live in his sight.
Then shall we know, if we follow on to know the Lord:
his going forth is prepared as the morning;
and he shall come unto us as the rain,
as the latter and former rain unto the earth.

—Hosea 6:1–3

Therefore also now, saith the Lord, turn ye even to me with all your heart, and with fasting, and with weeping, and with mourning: And rend your heart, and not your garments,  and turn unto the Lord your God: for he is gracious and merciful, slow to anger, and of great kindness, and repenteth him of the evil.

—Joel 2:12-13

Jonah's Prayer

*I cried by reason of mine affliction unto the Lord,
and he heard me; out of the belly of hell cried I,
and thou heardest my voice.
For thou hadst cast me into the deep, in the midst
of the seas; and the floods compassed me about:
all thy billows and thy waves passed over me.
Then I said, I am cast out of thy sight; yet I will look
again toward thy holy temple.
The waters compassed me about, even to the soul:
the depth closed me round about, the weeds were
wrapped about my head.
I went down to the bottoms of the mountains;
the earth with her bars was about me for ever:
yet hast thou brought up my life from corruption,
O Lord my God.
When my soul fainted within me I remembered
the Lord: and my prayer came in unto thee,
into thine holy temple.
They that observe lying vanities forsake their
own mercy.
But I will sacrifice unto thee with the voice of
thanksgiving; I will pay that that I have vowed.
Salvation is of the Lord.*

—Jonah 2:2–9

And the publican, standing afar off, would not lift
up so much as his eyes unto heaven,
but smote upon his breast, saying,
God be merciful to me a sinner.

—Luke 18:13

Then said Jesus, Father, forgive them;
for they know not what they do.

—Luke 23:34

During Times of Trial and Illness

When we need God the most, we know we can always call upon him in trust. That doesn't erase the pain we may feel in body, heart, or mind—but it does mean that we know that God is with us during our times of hardship and heartache.

As Above the Darkest Storm Cloud

As above the darkest storm cloud
Shines the sun, serenely bright
Waiting to restore to nature
All the glory of his light,
So, behind each cloud of sorrow,
So, in each affliction, stands,
Hid, an angel, with a blessing
From the Father in his hand.

—Daniel H. Howard

G od will never leave thee,
All thy wants He knows,
Feels the pains that grieve thee,
Sees thy cares and woes.
Raise thine eyes to heaven
When thy spirits quail,
When, by tempests driven,
Heart and courage fail.
When in grief we languish,
He will dry the tear,
Who His children's anguish
Soothes with succour near.
All our woe and sadness,
In this world below,
Balance not the gladness,
We in heaven shall know.

—General Hymn #286, Book of Common Prayer

There Is No Sorrow, Lord, Too Light

There is no sorrow, Lord, too light
  To bring in prayer to Thee;
There is no anxious care too slight
To wake Thy sympathy.
Thou, who hast trod the thorny road,
Wilt share each small distress;
The love which bore the greater load
Will not refuse the less.
There is no secret sigh we breathe
But meets Thine ear divine;
And every cross grows light beneath,
The shadow, Lord of Thine.

—Jane Crewdson

Heal us, Emmanuel, hear our prayer;
we wait to feel thy touch;
deep-wounded souls to thee repair,
and Savior, we are such.

—William Cowper

If your body suffers pain, and your health you can't
regain, and your soul is almost sinking in despair,
Jesus knows the pain you feel, he can save and he can
heal, take your burden to the Lord and leave it there.

—Charles Albert Tindley

Come, ye disconsolate, where'er ye languish;
Come, at the shrine of God fervently kneel;
Here bring your wounded hearts;
here tell your anguish;
Earth has no sorrow that heaven cannot heal.

—**Thomas Moore**

Have thine own way, Lord! Have thine own way!
Wounded and weary, help me I pray!
Power, all power, surely is thine!
Touch me and heal me, Savior divine!

—**Adelaide A. Pollard**

O Let Him Whose Sorrow

O let him whose sorrow
no relief can find,
Trust in God, and borrow
ease for the heart and mind.
Where the mourner weeping
sheds the secret tear,
God His watch is keeping,
though none else be near.
God will never leave thee,
All thy wants He knows,
Feels the pains that grieve thee,
sees thy cares and woes.
Raise thine eyes to Heaven
when thy spirits quail,
When, by tempests driven,
heart and courage fail.
All thy woe and sadness,
in this world below,
Balance not the gladness
thou in Heaven shalt know.

—**Heinrich Siegmund Oswald**

A Shelter in the Time of Storm

The raging storm may round us beat,
    A shelter in the time of storm;
We'll never leave our safe retreat,
A shelter in the time of storm.
Oh, Jesus is a Rock in a weary land,
A weary land, a weary land;
Oh, Jesus is a rock in a weary land,
A shelter in the time of storm.

—Vernon J. Charlesworth

The Eternal Goodness

Yet, in the maddening
maze of things,
And tossed by
storm and flood,
To one fixed trust
my spirit clings;
I know that God
is good!...
I know not
where His
islands lift
Their fronded
palms in air;
I only know
I cannot drift
Beyond His love and care.

—John Greenleaf Whittier

O magnify the Lord with me;
with me exalt his name;
when in distress to him I called,
he to my rescue came.
The hosts of God encamp around
the dwellings of the just;
deliverance he affords to all
who in his goodness trust.

—Nahum Tate

Lord, I am now in tribulation, and my heart is ill at ease, for I am much troubled with the present suffering. . . . Grant me patience, O Lord, even now in this moment. Help me, my God, and then I will not fear, how grievously soever I be afflicted.

—Thomas à Kempis

Psalm 6

O Lord, rebuke me not in thine anger,
neither chasten me in thy hot displeasure.
Have mercy upon me, O Lord; for I am weak:
O Lord, heal me; for my bones are vexed.
My soul is also sore vexed: but thou, O Lord,
how long?
Return, O Lord, deliver my soul: oh save me for
thy mercies' sake.
For in death there is no remembrance of thee:
in the grave who shall give thee thanks?
I am weary with my groaning; all the night make I
my bed to swim; I water my couch with my tears.
Mine eye is consumed because of grief;
it waxeth old because of all mine enemies.
Depart from me, all ye workers of iniquity;
for the Lord hath heard the voice of my weeping.
The Lord hath heard my supplication;
the Lord will receive my prayer.
Let all mine enemies be ashamed and sore vexed:
let them return and be ashamed suddenly.

Psalm 13

How long wilt thou forget me, O Lord? for ever? how long wilt thou hide thy face from me?
How long shall I take counsel in my soul, having sorrow in my heart daily?
How long shall mine enemy be exalted over me?
Consider and hear me, O Lord my God: lighten mine eyes, lest I sleep the sleep of death;
Lest mine enemy say, I have prevailed against him; and those that trouble me rejoice when I am moved.
But I have trusted in thy mercy; my heart shall rejoice in thy salvation.
I will sing unto the Lord, because he hath dealt bountifully with me.

Psalm 22

M y God, my God, why hast thou forsaken me?
why art thou so far from helping me, and from
the words of my roaring?
O my God, I cry in the day time, but thou hearest not;
and in the night season, and am not silent.
But thou art holy, O thou that inhabitest the praises
of Israel.
Our fathers trusted in thee: they trusted, and thou
didst deliver them.
They cried unto thee, and were delivered: they trusted
in thee, and were not confounded.

But I am a worm, and no man; a reproach of men,
and despised of the people.

All they that see me laugh me to scorn: they shoot out
the lip, they shake the head, saying,

He trusted on the Lord that he would deliver him:
let him deliver him, seeing he delighted in him.

But thou art he that took me out of the womb:
thou didst make me hope when I was upon my
mother's
breasts.

I was cast upon
thee from
the womb:
thou art my
God from my
mother's belly.
Be not far
from me;
for trouble is
near; for there
is none to help.
Many bulls
have
compassed me:

strong bulls of Bashan have beset me round.

They gaped upon me with their mouths, as a ravening
and a roaring lion.

I am poured out like water, and all my bones are out
of joint: my heart is like wax; it is melted in the midst
of my bowels.

My strength is dried up like a potsherd; and my tongue
cleaveth to my jaws; and thou hast brought me into the
dust of death.

For dogs have compassed me: the assembly of the wicked have inclosed me: they pierced my hands and my feet.

I may tell all my bones: they look and stare upon me.

They part my garments among them, and cast lots upon my vesture.

But be not thou far from me, O Lord: O my strength, haste thee to help me.

Deliver my soul from the sword; my darling from the power of the dog.

Save me from the lion's mouth: for thou hast heard me from the horns of the unicorns.

I will declare thy name unto my brethren: in the midst of the congregation will I praise thee.

Ye that fear the Lord, praise him; all ye the seed of

Jacob, glorify him; and fear him, all ye the seed of Israel. For he hath not despised nor abhorred the affliction of the afflicted; neither hath he hid his face

from him; but when he cried unto him, he heard.
My praise shall be of thee in the great congregation:
I will pay my vows before them that fear him.
The meek shall eat and be satisfied: they shall praise
the Lord that seek him: your heart shall live for ever.
All the ends of the world shall remember and turn unto
the Lord: and all the kindreds of the nations shall
worship before thee.
For the kingdom is the Lord's: and he is the governor
among the nations.
All they that be fat upon earth shall eat and worship:
all they that go down to the dust shall bow before him:
and none can keep alive his own soul.
A seed shall serve him; it shall be accounted to the
Lord for a generation.
They shall come, and shall declare his righteousness
unto a people that shall be born,
that he hath done this.

To every thing there is a season,
and a time to every purpose under the heaven:
A time to be born, and a time to die; a time to plant,
and a time to pluck up that which is planted;
A time to kill, and a time to heal;
a time to break down, and a time to build up;
A time to weep, and a time to laugh;
a time to mourn, and a time to dance;
A time to cast away stones, and a time to gather
stones together; a time to embrace,
and a time to refrain from embracing;
A time to get, and a time to lose;
a time to keep, and a time to cast away;
A time to rend, and a time to sew;
a time to keep silence, and a time to speak;
A time to love, and a time to hate;
a time of war, and a time of peace.

—Ecclesiastes 3:1-8

A Prayer of Elijah

And he cried unto the Lord, and said, O Lord my God, hast thou also brought evil upon the widow with whom I sojourn, by slaying her son?
And he stretched himself upon the child three times, and cried unto the Lord, and said, O Lord my God, I pray thee, let this child's soul come into him again. And the Lord heard the voice of Elijah; and the soul of the child came into him again, and he revived.

—1 Kings 17:20–22

A Prayer of Hezekiah

Then he turned his face to the wall, and prayed unto the Lord, saying, I beseech thee, O Lord, remember now how I have walked before thee in truth and with a perfect heart, and have done that which is good in thy sight. And Hezekiah wept sore.

—**2 Kings 20:2–3**

Heal me, O Lord, and I shall be healed; save me, and I shall be saved: for thou art my praise.

—**Jeremiah 17:14**

Although the fig tree shall not blossom,
neither shall fruit be in the vines; the labour of the
olive shall fail,
and the fields
shall yield no
meat; the flock
shall be cut off
from the fold,
and there shall
be no herd in
the stalls:
Yet I will
rejoice in the
Lord, I will joy
in the God of
my salvation.
The Lord God
is my strength,
and he will make my
feet like hinds' feet, and he will make me to walk
upon mine high places.

—Habakkuk 3:17-19

And lest I [Paul] should be exalted above measure through the abundance of the revelations, there was given to me a thorn in the flesh, the messenger of Satan to buffet me, lest I should be exalted above measure.

For this thing I besought the Lord thrice, that it might depart from me.

And he said unto me, My grace is sufficient for thee: for my strength is made perfect in weakness.

Most gladly therefore will I rather glory in my infirmities, that the power of Christ may rest upon me.

Therefore I take pleasure in infirmities, in reproaches, in necessities, in persecutions, in distresses for Christ's sake: for when I am weak, then am I strong.

—2 Corinthians 12:7–10

Lord, either lighten my burden or strengthen my back.

—Thomas Fuller

How often we look upon God as our last and feeblest resource! We go to him because we have nowhere else to go. And then we learn that the storms of life have driven us, not upon the rocks, but into the desired haven.

—George MacDonald

Abide with Me

Abide with me,
fast falls the eventide;
The darkness deepens;
Lord, with me abide!
When other helpers fail
And comforts flee,
Help of the helpless,
O abide with me.
I need thy presence
Every passing hour;
What but thy grace
Can foil the tempter's power?
Who like thyself,
My guide and stay can be?
Through cloud and sunshine,
Lord, abide, with me.

—Henry F. Lyte

Hope and Consolation

Hope is about believing with a humble heart that tomorrow can be different. It's about knowing that light will come to chase away this present darkness.

God, My Hope on You Is Founded

All my hope on God is founded
who will all my trust renew,
who through change and chance will guide me,
only good and only true.
God unknown,
God alone,
call my heart to
be thine own.

Mortal pride and
earthly glory,
sword and crown
betray our trust;
what with care
and toil we
fashion,
tow'r and
temple, fall to
dust. But thy
pow'r, hour
by hour, is my
temple and my tow'r.

Great thy goodness, e'er enduring;
deep thy wisdom, passing thought;

splendor, light, and life attend thee,
beauty springing out of naught.
Evermore from thy store
new-born worlds rise and adore.

Still from earth to God eternal
sacrifice of praise be done,
high above all praises praising
for the gift of God's own Son.
Christ doth call
one and all:
ye who follow shall not fall.

—Joachim Neander, trans. Robert Seymour Bridges

Lift Every Voice and Sing

Lift every voice and sing till earth and heaven ring,
ring with the harmonies of liberty;
let our rejoicing rise high as the listening skies,
let it resound loud as the rolling sea.
Sing a song full of the faith
that the dark past has taught us,
sing a song full of the hope
that the present has brought us;
facing the rising sun of our new day begun,
let us march on till victory is won.

—James Weldon Johnson

There Is a Balm in Gilead

There is a balm in Gilead
   To make the wounded whole;
There is a balm in Gilead
To heal the sin-sick soul.

Some times I feel discouraged,
And think my work's in vain,
But then the Holy Spirit
Revives my soul again.

If you can't preach like Peter,
If you can't pray like Paul,
Just tell the love of Jesus,
And say He died for all.

There is a balm in Gilead
To make the wounded whole;
There is a balm in Gilead
To heal the sin-sick soul.

—**Traditional African-American Spiritual**

Light Shining Out of Darkness

God moves in a mysterious way
His wonders to perform
He plants his footsteps in the sea
And rides upon the storm.
Deep in unfathomable mines
Of never-failing skill
He treasures up his bright designs,
And works his sovereign will.
Ye fearful saints fresh courage take;
The clouds ye so much dread
Are big with mercy, and shall break
In blessings on your head.

—William Cowper

Lord Jesus, you are medicine to me when I am sick, strength to me when I need help, life itself when I fear death, the way when I long for heaven, the light when all is dark, and food when I need nourishment. Glory be to you forever. Amen.

—St. Ambrose

Give to the Winds Thy Fears

Give to the winds thy fears
Hope and be undismayed;
God hears thy sighs and counts thy tears
God shall lift up thy head.

Through waves and clouds and storms,
He gently clears thy way.
Wait thou his time; so shall this night
Soon end in joyous day.

Let us in life, death,
They steadfast truth declare
And publish with our latest breath
Thy love and guardian care.

—Paul Gerhardt, translated by John Wesley

O God, Our Help in Ages Past

O God, our help in ages past,
Our hope for years to come;
Be Thou our guide while life shall last,
And our eternal home.

Under the shadow of thy throne,
Still may we dwell secure;
Sufficient is thine arm alone,
And our defense is sure.

—Isaac Watts

The Comforter Has Come

O spread the tidings 'round, wherever man is found,
wherever human hearts and human woes abound;
let every Christian tongue proclaim the joyful sound:
The Comforter has come!

The Comforter has come, the Comforter has come!
The Holy Ghost from heaven,
the Father's promise given;
O spread the tidings 'round, wherever man is found—
the Comforter has come!

The long, long night is past,
the morning breaks at last,
and hushed the dreadful wail and fury of the blast,
as over the golden hills the day advances fast!
The Comforter has come!

—Frank Bottome

Wonderful Words of Life

Christ, the blessed one, gives to all
Wonderful words of life;
Sinner heed now his loving call,
Wonderful words of life.
All so freely given,
Wooing us to heaven:
Beautiful words, wonderful words
Wonderful words of life.

—Phillip P. Bliss

Savior, Like a Shepherd Lead Us

Savior, like a shepherd lead us,
Much we need thy tender care;
In thy pleasant pastures feed us,
For our use thy folds prepare.
Blessed Jesus, blessed Jesus,
Thou hast bought us, thine we are.
Blessed Jesus, blessed Jesus,
Thou hast bought us, thine we are.

We are Thine, do Thou befriend us,
Be the guardian of our way;
Keep Thy flock, from sin defend us,
Seek us when we go astray:
Blessed Jesus, blessed Jesus,
Hear, O hear us when we pray;
Blessed Jesus, blessed Jesus,
Hear, O hear us when we pray.

—Dorothy A. Thrupp

Wade in the Water

Wade in the water
Wade in the water, children,
Wade in the water
God's a-going to trouble the water
See that host all dressed in white
God's a-going to trouble the water
The leader looks like the Israelite
God's a-going to trouble the water
See that band all dressed in red
God's a-going to trouble the water
Looks like the band that Moses led
God's a-going to trouble the water
Look over yonder, what do you see?
God's a-going to trouble the water
The Holy Ghost a-coming on me
God's a-going to trouble the water
If you don't believe I've been redeemed
God's a-going to trouble the water
Just follow me down to the Jordan's stream
God's a-going to trouble the water.

—**Traditional Spiritual**

Come, Thou long-expected Jesus,
Born to set thy people free;
From our fears and sin release us;
Let us find our rest in thee.

—Charles Wesley

*And the Lord shall guide thee continually,
and satisfy thy soul in drought, and make fat
thy bones: and thou shalt be like a watered garden,
and like a spring of water, whose waters fail not.*

—Isaiah 58:11

Psalm 11

In the Lord put I my trust: how say ye to my soul,
Flee as a bird to your mountain?
For, lo, the wicked bend their bow, they make ready
their arrow upon the string, that they may privily
shoot at the upright in heart.
If the foundations be destroyed,
what can the righteous do?
The Lord is in his holy temple, the Lord's throne
is in heaven: his eyes behold, his eyelids try,
the children of men.
The Lord trieth the righteous: but the wicked
and him that loveth violence his soul hateth.
Upon the wicked he shall rain snares,
fire and brimstone, and an horrible tempest:
this shall be the portion of their cup.
For the righteous Lord loveth righteousness;
his countenance doth behold the upright.

Psalm 23

The Lord is my shepherd; I shall not want.
He maketh me to lie down in green pastures:
he leadeth me beside the still waters.
He restoreth my soul: he leadeth me in the paths
of righteousness for his name's sake.
Yea, though I walk through the valley of the shadow
of death, I will fear no evil: for thou art with me;
thy rod and thy staff they comfort me.
Thou preparest a table before me in the presence
of mine enemies: thou anointest my head with oil;
my cup runneth over.
Surely goodness and mercy shall follow me all the
days of my life: and I will dwell in the house of the
Lord for ever.

Psalm 27

The Lord is my light and my salvation; whom shall I fear? The Lord is the strength of my life; of whom shall I be afraid?
When the wicked, even mine enemies and my foes, came upon me to eat up my flesh,
they stumbled and fell.
Though an host should encamp against me, my heart shall not fear: though war should rise against me, in this will I be confident.
One thing have I desired of the Lord, that will I seek after; that I may dwell in the house of the Lord all the days of my life, to behold the beauty of the Lord, and to enquire in his temple.
For in the time of trouble he shall hide me in his pavilion: in the secret of his tabernacle shall he hide me; he shall set me up upon a rock.
And now shall mine head be lifted up above mine enemies round about me: therefore will I offer in his tabernacle sacrifices of joy; I will sing, yea, I will sing praises unto the Lord.
Hear, O Lord, when I cry with my voice:
have mercy also upon me, and answer me.
When thou saidst, Seek ye my face; my heart said unto thee, Thy face, Lord, will I seek.

Hide not thy face far from me; put not thy servant
away in anger: thou hast been my help; leave me not,
neither forsake me, O God of my salvation.
When my father and my mother forsake me,
then the Lord will take me up.
Teach me thy way, O Lord, and lead me in a plain path,
because of mine enemies.
Deliver me not over unto the will of mine enemies:
for false witnesses are risen up against me,
and such as breathe out cruelty.
I had fainted, unless I had believed to see the goodness
of the Lord in the land of the living.
Wait on the Lord: be of good courage, and he shall
strengthen thine heart: wait, I say, on the Lord.

Psalm 46

God is our refuge and strength,
a very present help in trouble.
Therefore will not we fear, though the earth be
removed, and though the mountains be carried
into the midst of the sea;
Though the waters thereof roar and be troubled,
though the
mountains shake
with the swelling
thereof. Selah.
There is a river,
the streams where-
of shall make glad
the city of God,
the holy place of
the tabernacles of
the most High.
God is in the midst
of her; she shall
not be moved:
God shall help her,
and that right early.

The heathen raged, the kingdoms were moved:
he uttered his voice, the earth melted.

The Lord of hosts is with us; the God of Jacob is our refuge. Selah.
Come, behold the works of the Lord, what desolations he hath made in the earth.
He maketh wars to cease unto the end of the earth; he breaketh the bow, and cutteth the spear in sunder; he burneth the chariot in the fire.
Be still, and know that I am God: I will be exalted among the heathen, I will be exalted in the earth.
The Lord of hosts is with us; the God of Jacob is our refuge.

Psalm 121

I will lift up mine eyes unto the hills,
from whence cometh my help.
My help cometh from the Lord,
which made heaven and earth.
He will not suffer thy foot to be moved:
he that keepeth thee will not slumber.
Behold, he that keepeth Israel shall neither
slumber nor sleep.
The Lord is thy keeper: the Lord is thy shade
upon thy right hand.
The sun shall not smite thee by day,
nor the moon by night.
The Lord shall preserve thee from all evil:
he shall preserve thy soul.
The Lord shall preserve thy going out and thy coming
in from this time forth, and even for evermore.

And it shall come to pass in the last days,
that the mountain of the Lord's house shall be
established in the top of the mountains, and shall
be exalted above the hills; and all nations shall flow
unto it.
And many people shall go and say, Come ye,
and let us go up to the mountain of the Lord,
to the house of the God of Jacob; and he will teach
us of his ways, and we will walk in his paths:
for out of Zion shall go forth the law, and the word
of the Lord from Jerusalem.
And he shall judge among the nations, and shall
rebuke many people: and they shall beat their
swords into plowshares, and their spears into
pruninghooks: nation shall not lift up sword against
nation, neither shall they learn war any more.
O house of Jacob, come ye, and let us walk in the
light of the Lord.

—Isaiah 2:2-5

The people that walked in darkness have seen a
great light: they that dwell in the land of the
shadow of death, upon them hath the light shined.
Thou hast multiplied the nation, and not increased
the joy: they joy before thee according to the joy
in harvest, and as men rejoice when they divide
the spoil.
For thou hast broken the yoke of his burden,
and the staff of his shoulder, the rod of his
oppressor, as in the day of Midian.
For every battle of the warrior is with confused
noise, and garments rolled in blood;
but this shall be with burning and fuel of fire.
For unto us a child is born, unto us a son is given:
and the government shall be upon his shoulder:
and his name shall be called Wonderful, Counsellor,
The mighty God, The everlasting Father,
The Prince of Peace.

—Isaiah 9:2–6

The Lord is my portion, saith my soul; therefore will I hope in him. The Lord is good unto them that wait for him, to the soul that seeketh him. It is good that a man should both hope and quietly wait for the salvation of the Lord.

—**Lamentations 3:24-26**

Come unto me, all ye that labour and are heavy laden, and I will give you rest. Take my yoke upon you, and learn of me; for I am meek and lowly in heart: and ye shall find rest unto your souls. For my yoke is easy, and my burden is light.

—Matthew 11:28-30

And he said unto Jesus, Lord, remember me when thou comest into thy kingdom. And Jesus said unto him, Verily I say unto thee, Today shalt thou be with me in paradise.

—Luke 23:42-43

⟨⟨ᘒᘒ⟩⟩

B lessed be God, even the Father of our Lord Jesus Christ, the Father of mercies, and the God of all comfort;
Who comforteth us in all our tribulation, that we may be able to comfort them which are in any trouble, by the comfort wherewith we ourselves are comforted of God.
For as the sufferings of Christ abound in us, so our consolation also aboundeth by Christ.

—2 Corinthians 1:3-5

Trust

Proverbs 3:5-6 directs, "Trust in the Lord with all thine heart; and lean not unto thine own understanding. In all thy ways acknowledge him, and he shall direct thy paths." As we grow in faith, we grow to trust the Lord more deeply.

How Can I Keep from Singing?

My life flows on in endless song;
above earth's lamentation,
I catch the sweet, though far-off hymn
that hails a new creation.

No storm can shake my inmost calm
while to that Rock I'm clinging.
Since Christ is Lord of heaven and earth,
how can I keep from singing?

Through all the tumult and the strife,
I hear that music ringing.
It finds an echo in my soul.
How can I keep
from singing?

What though
my joys and
comforts die?
I know my
Savior liveth.
What though
the darkness
gather round?
Songs in
the night
he giveth.

The peace of
Christ makes fresh my heart,
a fountain ever springing!
All things are mine since I am his!
How can I keep from singing?

—Robert Lowry

His Eye Is on the Sparrow

Why should I feel discouraged,
    why should the shadows come,
Why should my heart be lonely,
and long for heav'n and home,
When Jesus is my portion? My constant Friend is He:
His eye is on the sparrow, and I know He watches me;
His eye is on the sparrow, and I know He watches me.

I sing because I'm happy,
I sing because I'm free,
For His eye is on the sparrow,
and I know He watches me.

"Let not your heart be troubled,"
His tender word I hear,
And resting on His goodness,
I lose my doubts and fears;
Though by the path He leadeth, but one step I may see;
His eye is on the sparrow, and I know He watches me;
His eye is on the sparrow, and I know He watches me.

—Civilla D. Martin

Prayer for God's Help

O God, from whom to be turned is to fall,
to whom to be turned is to rise,
and with whom to stand is to abide for ever;
grant us in all our duties your help,
in all our perplexities your guidance,
in all our dangers your protection,
and in all our sorrows your peace,
through Jesus Christ our Lord, Amen.

—St. Augustine

Jesus to His Disciples

I have instructed you to follow me
What way I go;
The road is hard, and stony—as I know;
Uphill it climbs, and from the crushing heat
No shelter will be found
Save in my shadow: wherefore follow me;
the footprints of my feet
Will be distinct and clear;
However trodden on, they will not disappear.

—Edna St. Vincent Millay

Hymn of Trust

T hough long the weary way we tread,
   And sorrow crown each lingering year,
No path we shun, no darkness dread,
Our hearts still whispering, thou art near!

—Oliver Wendell Holmes

I am weak, but thou art mighty;
  hold me with thy powerful hand.

—William Williams

Under His Wings

Under his wings I am safely abiding,
though the night deepens and tempests are wild;
still I can trust him, I know he will keep me,
he has redeemed me and I am his child.
Under his wings, under his wings,
who from his love can sever?
Under his wings my soul shall abide,
safely abide forever.
Under his wings, O what precious enjoyment!
There will I hide till life's trials are o'er;
sheltered, protected,
no evil can harm me,
resting in Jesus I'm safe evermore.
Under his wings, under his wings,
who from his love can sever?
Under his wings my soul shall abide,
safely abide forever.

—William O. Cushing

He's got you and me, brother, in his hands,
He's got you and me, sister, in his hands,
He's got all of us together in his hands,
He's got the whole world in his hands.

—Anonymous

Psalm 16

Preserve me, O God: for in thee do I put my trust.
O my soul, thou hast said unto the Lord,
Thou art my Lord: my goodness extendeth not to thee;
But to the saints that are in the earth,
and to the excellent, in whom is all my delight.

Their sorrows shall be multiplied that hasten after
another god: their drink offerings of blood will I not
offer, nor take up their names into my lips.
The Lord is the portion of mine inheritance and of

my cup: thou maintainest my lot.
The lines are fallen unto me in pleasant places;
yea, I have a goodly heritage.
I will bless the Lord, who hath given me counsel:
my reins also instruct me in the night seasons.
I have set the Lord always before me: because he is at
my right hand, I shall not be moved.
Therefore my heart is glad, and my glory rejoiceth:
my flesh also shall rest in hope.
For thou wilt not leave my soul in hell; neither wilt thou suffer thine Holy One to see corruption. Thou wilt shew me the path of life: in thy presence is fullness of joy; at thy right hand there are pleasures for evermore.

Psalm 71

In thee, O Lord, do I put my trust: let me never be put to confusion.

Deliver me in thy righteousness, and cause me to escape: incline thine ear unto me, and save me.

Be thou my strong habitation, whereunto I may continually resort: thou hast given commandment to save me; for thou art my rock and my fortress. Deliver me, O my God, out of the hand of the wicked, out of the hand of the unrighteous and cruel man.

For thou art my hope, O Lord God: thou art my trust from my youth.

By thee have I been holden up from the womb: thou art he that took me out of my mother's bowels: my praise shall be continually of thee.

I am as a wonder unto many; but thou art my strong refuge.

Let my mouth be filled with thy praise and with thy honour all the day.

Cast me not off in the time of old age; forsake me not when my strength faileth.

For mine enemies speak against me; and they that lay wait for my soul take counsel together,

Saying, God hath forsaken him: persecute and take him; for there is none to deliver him.

O God, be not far from me: O my God, make haste for my help.

Let them be confounded and consumed that are adversaries to my soul; let them be covered with reproach and dishonour that seek my hurt.

But I will hope continually, and will yet praise thee more and more.

My mouth shall shew forth thy righteousness and thy salvation all the day; for I know not the numbers thereof.

I will go in the strength of the Lord God: I will make mention of thy righteousness, even of thine only.

O God, thou hast taught me from my youth: and hitherto have I declared thy wondrous works.

Now also when I am old and greyheaded, O God, forsake me not; until I have shewed thy strength unto this generation, and thy power to every one that is to come.

Thy righteousness also, O God, is very high, who hast done great things: O God, who is like unto thee!

Thou, which hast shewed me great and sore troubles, shalt quicken me again, and shalt bring me up again from the depths of the earth.

Thou shalt increase my greatness, and comfort me on every side.

I will also praise thee with the psaltery, even thy truth, O my God: unto thee will I sing with the harp, O thou Holy One of Israel.

My lips shall greatly rejoice when I sing unto thee; and my soul, which thou hast redeemed.

My tongue also shall talk of thy righteousness all the day long: for they are confounded, for they are brought unto shame, that seek my hurt.

Psalm 91

He that dwelleth in the secret place of the most High shall abide under the shadow of the Almighty.
I will say of the Lord, He is my refuge and my fortress: my God; in him will I trust.
Surely he shall deliver thee from the snare of the fowler, and from the noisome pestilence.
He shall cover thee with his feathers, and under his wings shalt thou trust: his truth shall be thy shield and buckler.
Thou shalt not be afraid for the terror by night; nor for the arrow that flieth by day;
Nor for the pestilence that walketh in darkness; nor for the destruction that wasteth at noonday.
A thousand shall fall at thy side, and ten thousand at thy right hand; but it shall not come nigh thee.
Only with thine eyes shalt thou behold and see the reward of the wicked.
Because thou hast made the Lord, which is my refuge, even the most High, thy habitation;
There shall no evil befall thee, neither shall any plague come nigh thy dwelling.
For he shall give his angels charge over thee, to keep thee in all thy ways.
They shall bear thee up in their hands,

lest thou dash thy foot against a stone.

Thou shalt tread upon the lion and adder: the young lion and the dragon shalt thou trample under feet.

Because he hath set his love upon me, therefore will I deliver him: I will set him on high, because he hath known my name.

He shall call upon me, and I will answer him: I will be with him in trouble; I will deliver him, and honour him.

With long life will I satisfy him, and shew him my salvation.

Behold, God is my salvation; I will trust,
and not be afraid: for the Lord Jehovah is
my strength and my song; he also is become my
salvation. Therefore with joy shall ye draw water
out of the wells of salvation.

—Isaiah 12:2–3

And when Jesus had cried with a loud voice,
he said, Father, into thy hands I commend my
spirit: and having said thus, he gave up the ghost.

—Luke 23:46

Growing Near to God

We are all seekers, trying to deepen our relationship with and understanding of God. In prayer, we open our hearts to the Lord, drawing near to him and opening ourselves to his presence. The prayers in this section focus on the need we have for and the delight we take in God's presence.

When I Survey the Wondrous Cross

When I survey the wondrous cross
on which the Prince of glory died,
my richest gain I count but loss,
and pour contempt on all my pride.

Forbid it, Lord, that I should boast
save in the death of Christ, my God!
All the vain things that charm me most,
I sacrifice them through his blood.

See, from his head, his hands, his feet,
sorrow and love flow mingled down.
Did e'er such love and sorrow meet,
or thorns compose so rich a crown?

Were the whole realm of nature mine,
that were a present far too small.
Love so amazing, so divine,
demands my soul, my life, my all.

—Isaac Watts

Come, Thou Fount of Every Blessing

Come, thou Fount of every blessing,
tune my heart to sing thy grace;
streams of mercy, never ceasing,
call for songs of loudest praise.
Teach me some melodious sonnet,
sung by flaming tongues above.
Praise the mount I'm fixed upon it
mount of God's
redeeming love.

Here I find my
greatest treasure;
hither by thy
help I've come;
and I hope,
by thy good
pleasure,
safely to arrive
at home.
Jesus sought me
when a stranger,
wandering from
the fold of God;
he, to rescue me
from danger,
bought me with his precious blood.

Oh, to grace how great a debtor
daily I'm constrained to be!
Let thy goodness, like a fetter,
bind my wandering heart to thee:
prone to wander, Lord, I feel it,
prone to leave the God I love;
here's my heart, O take and seal it;
seal it for thy courts above.

—Robert Robinson

Amazing Grace

Amazing grace how sweet the sound
that saved a wretch like me!
I once was lost but now am found,
was blind but now I see.

'Twas grace that taught my heart to fear,
and grace my fears relieved;
how precious did that grace appear
the hour I first believed!

The Lord has promised good to me,
his word my hope secures;
he will my shield and portion be
as long as life endures.

Through many dangers, toils, and snares
I have already come;
'tis grace hath brought me safe thus far,
and grace will lead me home.

When we've been there ten thousand years,
bright shining as the sun,
we've no less days to sing God's praise
than when we'd first begun.

—John Newton

O Love of God, descend into my heart;
Enlighten the dark corners of this neglected dwelling,
And scatter there Your cheerful beams.
Dwell in the soul that longs to be Your temple;
Water that barren soil overrun with weeds
and briars
And lost for lack of cultivating.
Make it fruitful with Your dew.
Come, dear Refreshment of those who languish;
come, Star and Guide of those who sail
amidst tempests.
You are Haven of the tossed and shipwrecked.
Come now, Glory and Crown of the living,
As well as the Safeguard of the dying.
Come, Sacred Spirit;
Come, and make me fit to receive You.

—St. Augustine

O gracious and holy Father,
Give us wisdom to perceive you,
intelligence to understand you,
diligence to seek you,
patience to wait for you,
eyes to see you,
a heart to meditate on you,
and a life to proclaim you,
through the power of the spirit of
Jesus Christ our Lord.

—St. Benedict

In the Garden

I come to the garden alone while the dew
is still on the roses
And the voice I hear falling on my ear
the Son of God discloses
And he walks with me, and he talks with me
And he tells me I am His own
And the joy we share as we tarry there
None other has ever known.

—C. Austin Miles

Our Weakness, Your Strength

There is much to drag us back, O Lord:
empty pursuits, trivial pleasures, unworthy cares.
There is much to frighten us away: pride that makes
us reluctant to accept help; cowardice that recoils from
sharing your suffering; anguish at the prospect of
confessing our sins to you. But you are stronger than
all these forces. We call you our redeemer and saviour
because you redeem us from our empty, trivial
existence, you save us from our foolish fears.
This is your work, which you have completed
and will continue to complete every moment.

—Søren Kierkegaard

Draw Me into Yourself

Draw me completely into yourself,
So that I might completely melt in your love.
Lay upon me, stamp upon me,
So that my stubborn pride might be destroyed.
Embrace me, kiss me,
So that my spiritual ugliness may turn to beauty.
Lock me into your chamber,
So that I might never stray from your presence.

—Johann Freylinghausen

Prayer of Abandonment

Father, I abandon myself into your hands;
do with me what you will.
Whatever you may do, I thank you:
I am ready for all, I accept all.
Let only your will be done in me,
and in all your creatures—
I wish no more than this, O Lord.

—Charles de Foucauld

Prayer to the Holy Spirit

Breathe in me, O Holy Spirit, that my thoughts may all be holy. Act in me, O Holy Spirit, that my work, too, may be holy. Draw my heart, O Holy Spirit, that I love but what is holy. Strengthen me, O Holy Spirit, to defend all that is holy. Guard me, then, O Holy Spirit, that I always may be holy. Amen.

—St. Augustine

Let us therefore desire nothing else, wish for nothing else, and let nothing please and delight us except our Creator and Redeemer, and Savior, the only true God, who is full of good, who alone is good, ...and from whom, and through whom, and in whom is all mercy, all grace, all glory of all penitents and of the just, and of all the blessed rejoicing in heaven.

—St. Francis of Assisi

Nearer to Thee

Though like the wanderer,
　The sun gone down,
Darkness be over me,
My rest a stone;
Yet in my dreams I'd be
Nearer, my God, to Thee,
Nearer to Thee!
...Then, with my waking thoughts
Bright with Thy praise,
out of my stony griefs,
Bethel I'll raise;
So by my woes to be
Nearer, my God, to Thee,
Nearer to Thee!

—Sarah Flower Adams

The Child of glory,
The Child of Mary,
Born in the stable,
The King of all,
Who came to the wilderness
And in our stead suffered;
Happy they are counted
Who to him are near.

—Celtic Traditional

God be in my head, and in my understanding;
God be in my eyes, and in my looking;
God be in my mouth, and in my speaking;
God be in my heart, and in my thinking;
God be at my end, and at my departing.

—Old Sarum Primer

Open My Eyes That I May See

Open my eyes that I may see
Glimpses of truth thou sendest me;
Place in my hands the wonderful key
That shall unclasp, and set me free:
Silently now I wait for thee,
Ready, my God, thy will to see;
Open my eyes, illumine me, Spirit divine!

Open my ears that I may hear
Voices of truth thou sendest clear;
And while the wavenotes fall on my ear,
Ev'rything false will disappear:
Silently now I wait for thee,
Ready my God, thy will to see;
Open my heart illumine me, Spirit divine!

—Clara H. Scott

I Need Thee Every Hour

I need thee ev'ry hour, Most gracious Lord;
No tender voice like thine Can peace afford.
I need thee ev'ry hour, Stay thou near by;
Temptations lose their pow'r When thou art nigh.
I need thee ev'ry hour, In joy or pain;
Come quickly and abide, Or life is vain.
I need thee ev'ry hour, Teach me thy will;
Thy promises so rich, In me fulfill.
I need thee ev'ry hour, Most Holy One
O make me thine indeed, Thou blessed Son.
I need thee, O I need thee;
Ev'ry hour I need!
O bless me now, My Savior,
I come to thee.
Amen.

—Annie S. Hawks

Come, thou Holy Spirit, come;
And from Thy celestial home
Shed a ray of light Divine:
Come, Thou Father of the poor,
Come, Thou source of all our store,
Come, within our bosoms shine:
Thou of Comforters the best,
Thou the soul's most welcome guest,
Sweet refreshment here below:
In our labour rest most sweet,
Grateful coolness in the heat,
Solace in the midst of woe.
O most Blessed Light Divine,
Shine within these hearts of Thine,
And our inmost being fill:
Where Thou art not, man hath nought,
Nothing good in deed or thought,
Nothing free from taint of ill.

—Whitsuntide, *Book of Common Prayer*,
Church of England

Where there is charity and wisdom,
there is neither fear nor ignorance.
Where there is patience and humility,
there is neither anger nor vexation.
Where there is poverty and joy,
there is neither greed nor avarice.
Where there is peace and meditation,
there is neither anxiety nor doubt.

—St. Francis of Assisi

Be Thou My Vision

Be thou my vision, O Lord of my heart;
Naught be all else to me, save that thou art:
Thou my best thought, by day and by night,
Walking or sleeping, thy presence my light.
Riches I heed not, or man's empty praise,
Thou mine inheritance, now and always:
Thou and thou only, first in my heart,
High King of heaven, my treasure thou art.

**—Traditional Irish, trans. Mary E. Byrne,
adapted Eleanor Hull**

Teach me, teach me, dearest Jesus
In thine own sweet loving, way,
All the lessons of perfection
I must practice day by day.
Teach me meekness, dearest Jesus,
Of Thine own the counterpart;
Not in words and actions only,
But the meekness of the heart.
Teach, Humility, sweet Jesus
To this poor, proud heart of mine,
Which yet wishes, O my Jesus,
To be modeled after Thine.

—Reverend F. X. Lasance

Lord, speak to me, that I may speak
In living echoes of thy tone;
As thou hast sought so let me seek
Thy erring children lost and lone.

O teach me, Lord, that I may teach
The precious things thou dost impart;
And wing my words, that they may reach
The hidden depths of many a heart.
O fill me with thy fullness, Lord,
Until my very heart o'erflow
In kindling thought and glowing word,
Thy love to tell, thy praise to show.

—**Frances Ridley Havergal**

Open wide the window of our spirits, O Lord, and fill us full of light; Open wide the door of our hearts, that we may receive and entertain thee with all our powers of adoration and love.

—Christina Rossetti

O Light that foll'west all my way, I yield my flickering torch to thee; my heart restores its borrowed ray, that in thy sunshine's blaze its day may brighter, fairer be.

—George Matheson

Walk in the Light

Walk in the light! So you shall know
that fellowship of love.
His Spirit only can bestow,
who reigns in light above.

Walk in the light! And you shall find
your heart made truly his,
who dwells in cloudless light enshrined,
in whom no darkness is.

Walk in the light! And yours shall be
a path, though thorny, bright.
For God, by grace, shall dwell in thee,
and God himself is light.

—Bernard Barton, Adapted

Take My Life and Let It Be

Take my life,
and let it be
consecrated,
Lord, to thee;
take my
moments
and my days;
let them flow in
ceaseless praise.
Take my hands,
and let them
move at the
impulse of
thy love.
Take my feet,
and let them be
swift and beautiful for thee.
Take my love, my Lord, I pour
at thy feet its treasure store.
Take myself, and I will be
ever, only, all for thee.

—Frances Ridley Havergal

L ord, grant me a simple, kind, open, believing, loving and generous heart, worthy of being your dwelling place.

—**John Sergieff**

O Lord never suffer us to think that we can stand by ourselves, and not need thee.

—**John Donne**

O God, we give thanks that your Son Jesus Christ, who has shared our earthly life, has now ascended to prepare our heavenly life. Grant that, through coming to know him by faith on earth, we may come to know him by sight in heaven.

—The Gelasian Sacramentary

A Prayer of David

Then went king David in, and sat before the Lord, and he said, Who am I, O Lord God? and what is my house, that thou hast brought me hitherto?
And this was yet a small thing in thy sight, O Lord God; but thou hast spoken also of thy servant's house for a great while to come. And is this the manner of man, O Lord God?
And what can David say more unto thee? for thou, Lord God, knowest thy servant.
For thy word's sake, and according to thine own heart, hast thou done all these great things, to make thy servant know them.
Wherefore thou art great, O Lord God: for there is none like thee, neither is there any God beside thee, according to all that we have heard with our ears.
And what one nation in the earth is like thy people, even like Israel, whom God went to redeem for a people to himself, and to make him a name, and to do for you great things and terrible, for thy land, before thy people, which thou redeemedst to thee from Egypt, from the nations and their gods?
For thou hast confirmed to thyself thy people Israel to be a people unto thee for ever: and thou, Lord, art become their God.
And now, O Lord God, the word that thou hast spoken

concerning thy servant, and concerning his house,
establish it for ever, and do as thou hast said.
And let thy name be magnified for ever, saying,
The Lord of hosts is the God over Israel: and let the
house of thy servant David be established before thee.
For thou, O Lord of hosts, God of Israel, hast revealed
to thy servant, saying, I will build thee an house:
therefore hath thy servant found in his heart to pray
this prayer unto thee.
And now, O Lord God, thou art that God, and thy
words be true, and thou hast promised this goodness
unto thy servant:
Therefore now let it please thee to bless the house of
thy servant, that it may continue for ever before thee:
for thou, O Lord God, hast spoken it: and with thy
blessing let the house of thy servant be blessed
for ever.

—2 Samuel 7:18-29

Psalm 1

Blessed is the man that walketh not in the counsel of the ungodly, nor standeth in the way of sinners, nor sitteth in the seat of the scornful.
But his delight is in the law of the Lord;
and in his law doth he meditate day and night.
And he shall be like a tree planted by the rivers of water, that bringeth forth his fruit in his season;
his leaf also shall not wither; and whatsoever he doeth shall prosper.
The ungodly are not so: but are like the chaff which the wind driveth away.
Therefore the ungodly shall not stand in the judgment, nor sinners in the congregation of the righteous.
For the Lord knoweth the way of the righteous:
but the way of the ungodly shall perish.

Psalm 42

As the hart panteth after the water brooks, so panteth my soul after thee, O God. My soul thirsteth for God, for the living God: when shall I come and appear before God? My tears have been my meat day and night, while they continually say unto me, Where is thy God?

When I remember these things, I pour out my soul in me: for I had gone with the multitude, I went with them to the house of God, with the voice of joy and praise, with a multitude that kept holy day.

Why art thou cast down, O my soul? and why art thou disquieted in me? hope thou in God: for I shall yet praise him for the help of his countenance.

O my God, my soul is cast down within me:
therefore will I remember thee from the land of Jordan,
and of the Hermonites, from the hill Mizar.
Deep calleth unto deep at the noise of thy waterspouts:
all thy waves and thy billows are gone over me.
Yet the Lord will command his lovingkindness in the
day time, and in the night his song shall be with me,
and my prayer unto the God of my life.
I will say unto God my rock, Why hast thou forgotten
me? why go I mourning because of the oppression of
the enemy?
As with a sword in my bones, mine enemies reproach
me; while they say daily unto me, Where is thy God?
Why art thou cast down, O my soul? and why art thou
disquieted within me? hope thou in God: for I shall yet
praise him, who is the health of my countenance,
and my God.

Psalm 63

OGod, thou art my God; early will I seek thee:
my soul thirsteth for thee, my flesh longeth for
thee in a dry and thirsty land, where no water is;
To see thy power and thy glory, so as I have seen thee
in the sanctuary.
Because thy lovingkindness is better than life,
my lips shall praise thee.
Thus will I bless thee while I live:
I will lift up my hands in thy name.

My soul shall be satisfied as with marrow and fatness;
and my mouth shall praise thee with joyful lips:
When I remember thee upon my bed,
and meditate on thee in the night watches.
Because thou hast been my help, therefore in the
shadow of thy wings will I rejoice.
My soul followeth hard after thee:
thy right hand upholdeth me.
But those that seek my soul, to destroy it,
shall go into the lower parts of the earth.
They shall fall
by the sword:
they shall be
a portion
for foxes.
But the king
shall rejoice in
God; every one
that sweareth
by him shall
glory: but the
mouth of them
that speak
lies shall
be stopped.

Psalm 84

How amiable are thy tabernacles, O Lord of hosts! My soul longeth, yea, even fainteth for the courts of the Lord: my heart and my flesh crieth out for the living God. Yea, the sparrow hath found an house, and the  swallow a nest for herself, where she may lay her young, even thine altars, O Lord of hosts, my King, and my God.

Blessed are they that dwell in thy house: they will be still praising thee. Selah.

Blessed is the man whose strength is in thee; in whose heart are the ways of them.

Who passing through the valley of Baca make it a well; the rain also filleth the pools.

They go from strength to strength, every one of them

in Zion appeareth before God.
O Lord God of hosts, hear my prayer: give ear, O God
of Jacob. Selah.
Behold, O God our shield, and look upon the face
of thine anointed.
For a day in thy courts is better than a thousand.
I had rather be a doorkeeper in the house of my God,
than to dwell in the tents of wickedness.
For the Lord God is a sun and shield: the Lord will give
grace and glory: no good thing will he withhold from
them that walk uprightly.
O Lord of hosts, blessed is the man that trusteth
in thee.

Psalm 122

I was glad when they said unto me,
Let us go into the house of the Lord.
Our feet shall stand within thy gates, O Jerusalem.
Jerusalem is builded as a city that is compact together:
Whither the tribes go up, the tribes of the Lord,
unto the testimony of Israel, to give thanks unto
the name of the Lord.
For there are set thrones of judgment, the thrones
of the house of David.
Pray for the peace of Jerusalem: they shall prosper
that love thee.
Peace be within thy walls, and prosperity within
thy palaces.
For my brethren and companions' sakes, I will now
say, Peace be within thee.
Because of the house of the Lord our God I will
seek thy good.

Psalm 139

O Lord, thou hast searched me, and known me.
Thou knowest my downsitting and mine uprising,
thou understandest my thought afar off.
Thou compassest my path and my lying down,
and art acquainted with all my ways.
For there is not a word in my tongue, but, lo, O Lord,
thou knowest it altogether.
Thou hast beset me behind and before, and laid thine
hand upon me.
Such knowledge is too wonderful for me; it is high,
I cannot attain unto it.

Whither shall I go from thy spirit? or whither shall I flee from thy presence?

If I ascend up into heaven, thou art there: if I make my bed in hell, behold, thou art there.

If I take the wings of the morning, and dwell in the uttermost parts of the sea;

Even there shall thy hand lead me, and thy right hand shall hold me.

If I say, Surely the darkness shall cover me; even the night shall be light about me.

Yea, the darkness hideth not from thee; but the night shineth as the day: the darkness and the light are both alike to thee.

For thou hast possessed my reins: thou hast covered me in my mother's womb.

I will praise thee; for I am fearfully and wonderfully made: marvellous are thy works; and that my soul knoweth right well.

My substance was not hid from thee, when I was made in secret, and curiously wrought in the lowest parts of the earth.

Thine eyes did see my substance, yet being unperfect; and in thy book all my members were written, which in continuance were fashioned, when as yet there was none of them.

How precious also are thy thoughts unto me, O God! how great is the sum of them!

If I should count them, they are more in number than the sand: when I awake, I am still with thee.

Surely thou wilt slay the wicked, O God: depart from me therefore, ye bloody men.

For they speak against thee wickedly, and thine enemies take thy name in vain.

Do not I hate them, O Lord, that hate thee? and am not I grieved with those that rise up against thee?

I hate them with perfect hatred: I count them mine enemies.

Search me, O God, and know my heart: try me, and know my thoughts:

And see if there be any wicked way in me, and lead me in the way everlasting.

J *esus answered and said unto her,*
Whosoever drinketh of this water
shall thirst again:
But whosoever drinketh of the water that I shall
give him shall never thirst; but the water that
I shall give him shall be in him a well of water
springing up into everlasting life.

—John 4:13-14

Responding to God's Call

W e cherish the Bible stories of the prophets and disciples who responded to God's call to serve him. Some responded promptly, like the apostles who left their nets to follow Jesus; others, like Moses, protested that they had some flaw that left them unfit for the role. Through their examples, we know that we are all called to serve God and do his will in serving our brothers and sisters.

Teach us, good Lord, to serve Thee
as Thou deservest.
To give and not to count the cost:
To fight and not to heed the wounds:
To toil and not to seek for rest:
To labour and not to ask for any reward
Save that of knowing that we do thy will.

—St. Ignatius Loyola

Deliver me, O God, from a slothful mind, from all lukewarmness, and all dejection of spirit. I know these cannot but deaden my love to you; mercifully free my heart from them, and give me a lively, zealous, active, and cheerful spirit, that I may vigorously perform whatever you command, thankfully suffer whatever you choose for me, and be ever ardent to obey in all things your holy love.

—John Wesley

Joy is not gush; joy is not jolliness. Joy is perfect acquiescence in God's will because the soul delights in God himself.

—H. W. Webb-Peploe

Be the eye of God dwelling with you
The foot of Christ in guidance with you
The shower of the Spirit pouring on you
Richly and generously.

—Alexander Carmichael

Little drops of water,
Little grains of sand,
Make the mighty ocean
And the pleasant land.
Little deeds of kindness,
Little words of love,
Help to make earth happy
Like the heaven above.

—Julia Fletcher Carney

D o all the good you can,
By all the means you can,
In all the ways you can,
In all the places you can,
At all the times you can,
To all the people you can,
As long as ever you can.

—John Wesley

Lord, make me an instrument of your peace;
where there is hatred, let me sow love;
where there is injury, pardon;
where there is doubt, faith;
where there is despair, hope;
where there is darkness, light;
and where there is sadness, joy.
Divine Master, grant that I may not so much seek
to be consoled as to console;
to be understood as to understand;
to be loved as to love.
For it is in giving that we receive,
it is in pardoning that we are pardoned,
and it is in dying that we are born to eternal life.

—St. Francis of Assisi

Blest Be the Tie That Binds

Blest be the tie that binds
our hearts in Christian love;
the fellowship of kindred minds
is like to that above.
Before our Father's throne
we pour our ardent prayers;
our fears, our hopes, our aims are one,
our comforts and our cares.
When we asunder part,
it gives us inward pain,
but we shall still be joined in heart,
and hope to meet again.

—Rev. John Fawcett

Psalm 15

Lord, who shall abide in thy tabernacle?
who shall dwell in thy holy hill?
He that walketh uprightly, and worketh righteousness,
and speaketh the truth in his heart.
He that backbiteth not with his tongue,
nor doeth evil to his neighbour,
nor taketh up a reproach against his neighbour.
In whose eyes a vile person is contemned;
but he honoureth them that fear the Lord.
He that sweareth to his own hurt, and changeth not.
He that putteth not out his money to usury,
nor taketh reward against the innocent.
He that doeth these things shall never be moved.

Call to me and I will answer you, and will tell you great and hidden things that you have not known.

—Jeremiah 33:3

Also I heard the voice of the Lord, saying, Whom shall I send, and who will go for us? Then said I, Here am I; send me.

—Isaiah 6:8

*I*s not this the fast that I have chosen?
to loose the bands of wickedness, to undo the
heavy burdens, and to let the oppressed go free,
and that ye break every yoke?
Is it not to deal thy bread to the hungry,
and that thou bring the poor that are cast out to
thy house? when thou seest the naked, that thou
cover him; and that thou hide not thyself from
thine own flesh?
Then shall thy light break forth as the morning,
and thine health shall spring forth speedily:
and thy righteousness shall go before thee;
the glory of the Lordshall be thy reward.
Then shalt thou call, and the Lord shall answer;
thou shalt cry, and he shall say, Here I am.
If thou take away from the midst of thee the yoke,
the putting forth of the finger,
and speaking vanity;
And if thou draw out thy soul to the hungry,
and satisfy the afflicted soul; then shall thy
light rise in obscurity, and thy darkness be
as the noon day.

—Isaiah 58:6-10

S eek good, and not evil, that ye may live:
and so the Lord, the God of hosts,
shall be with you, as ye have spoken.

—Amos 5:14

H e hath shewed thee, O man, what is good;
and what doth the Lord require of thee,
but to do justly, and to love mercy,
and to walk humbly with thy God?

—Micah 6:8

A nd he said, Abba, Father, all things are possible unto thee; take away this cup from me: nevertheless not what I will, but what thou wilt.

—Mark 14:36

A nd Mary said, Behold the handmaid of the Lord; be it unto me according to thy word. And the angel departed from her.

—Luke 1:38

Prayer

Just when all seems hopeless, prayer lifts us like a wave on the ocean. A sturdy craft, prayer doesn't hide from pain, but uses it like the force of the sea to move us to a new place of insight, patience, courage, and sympathy. Always, it is God's hand beneath the surface holding us up.

Every Time I Feel the Spirit

E very time I feel the Spirit
moving in my heart I will pray.
Yes, every time I feel the Spirit
moving in my heart I will pray.

—Traditional African-American spiritual

Pray without ceasing,
let your love illumine the skies
That the darkness of man may drop away
And only the light of God show through.
Pray unto the Holy, with all your heart and soul
Pray for the shining light of guidance
That your path may be glorious with love.

—St. Augustine

Prayer is a great weapon, a rich treasure, a wealth
that is never exhausted, an undisturbed refuge,
a cause of tranquility, the root of a multitude of
blessings, and their source.

—St. John Chrysostom

What a Friend We Have in Jesus

What a friend we have in Jesus,
　All our sins and griefs to bear!
What a privilege to carry
Everything to God in prayer!
O what peace we often forfeit,
O what needless pain we bear,
All because we do not carry
Everything to God in prayer!

Have we trials and temptations?
Is there trouble anywhere?
We should never be discouraged,
Take it to the Lord in prayer.
Can we find a friend so faithful
Who will all our sorrows share?
Jesus knows our every weakness,
Take it to the Lord in prayer.

—Joseph M. Scriven

Sweet Hour of Prayer

Sweet hour of prayer, sweet hour of prayer,
That calls me from a world of care
And bids me at my Father's throne
Make all my wants and wishes known!
In seasons of distress and grief,
My soul has often found relief,
And oft escaped the tempter's snare
By thy return, sweet hour of prayer.

—Joseph M. Scriven

The day was long, the burden I had borne
Seemed heavier that I could no longer bear;
And then it lifted—but I did not know
Someone had knelt in prayer.
Had taken me to God that very hour,
And asked the easing of the load,
and He in infinite compassion,
had stooped down
And lifted the burden from me.
We cannot tell how often as we pray
For some bewildered one, hurt and distressed,
The answer comes, but many times these hearts
Find sudden peace and rest.
Someone had prayed, and faith, a lifted hand
Reached up to God,
and He reached down that day.
So many, many hearts have need of prayer—
Then, let us, let us pray.

—**Author Unknown**

No one should give the answer that it is impossible for a man occupied with worldly cares to pray always. You can set up an altar to God in your mind by means of prayer. And so it is fitting to pray at your trade, on a journey, standing at a counter or sitting at your handicraft.

—St. John Chrysostom

Speak, move, act in peace, as if you were in prayer. In truth, this is prayer.

—Francois de Salignace de La Mothe Fenelon

Prayer is a powerful thing, for God has bound and tied himself thereto. None can believe how powerful prayer is, and what it is able to effect, but those who have learned it by experience.

—**Martin Luther**

He prayeth best who loveth best all things both great and small; for the dear God who loveth us, He made and loveth all.

—**Samuel Taylor Coleridge**

Prayer (I)

Prayer the church's banquet, angel's age,
  God's breath in man returning to his birth,
 The soul in paraphrase, heart in pilgrimage,
The Christian plummet sounding heav'n and earth
Engine against th' Almighty, sinner's tow'r,
 Reversed thunder, Christ-side-piercing spear,
The six-days world transposing in an hour,
A kind of tune, which all things hear and fear;
Softness, and peace, and joy, and love, and bliss,
 Exalted manna, gladness of the best,
 Heaven in ordinary, man well drest,
The milky way, the bird of Paradise,
 Church-bells beyond the stars heard, the soul's blood,
The land of spices; something understood.

—George Herbert

I f you pray truly, you will feel within yourself a great assurance, and the angels will be your companions.

—Evagrius of Pontus

B etween the humble and contrite heart and the mystery of heaven there are no barriers; the only password is prayer.

—Hosea Ballou

P rayer is the mother and daughter of tears. It is an expiation of sin, a bridge across temptation, a bulwark against affliction. It wipes out conflict, is the work of angels, and is the nourishment of everything spiritual.

—St. John Climacus, *The Ladder of Divine Ascent*

The Lord's Prayer

And when thou prayest, thou shalt not be as the hypocrites are: for they love to pray standing in the synagogues and in the corners of the streets, that they may be seen of men. Verily I say unto you, They have their reward.

But thou, when thou prayest, enter into thy closet, and when thou hast shut thy door, pray to thy Father which is in secret; and thy Father which seeth in secret shall reward thee openly.

But when ye pray, use not vain repetitions, as the heathen do: for they think that they shall be heard for their much speaking.

Be not ye therefore like unto them: for your Father knoweth what things ye have need of, before ye ask him.

After this manner therefore pray ye: Our Father which art in heaven, Hallowed be thy name.

Thy kingdom come, Thy will be done in earth, as it is in heaven.

Give us this day our daily bread.

And forgive us our debts, as we forgive our debtors.

And lead us not into temptation, but deliver us from evil: For thine is the kingdom, and the power, and the glory, for ever. Amen.

—Matthew 6:5-13